# Burn
# Loot
# Murder

## The Truth About Black Live
## Matter and Their Radical Agenda

Burn Loot Murder: The Truth About Black Lives Matter and Their Radical Agenda

Copyright © 2020 B. L. M.

To all patriotic Americans who are tired of
extremist groups tearing us apart.

# Contents

# Burn

# Loot

# Murder

## The Truth About Black Lives Matter and Their Radical Agenda

B. L. M.

# Introduction

*Communism is not love. Communism is a hammer*
*which we use to crush the enemy.—Mao Zedong*

Black Lives Matter (BLM), the self-proclaimed promoter of black rights and racial justice in this country, seems to have come out of nowhere and have since become a political party with real political power. But how did they accomplish so much in such a short amount of time? Why is it they are listened to as though they are an authority on what constitutes racism and racial justice? Where did they come from? Who funds them? How did they garner such a huge following and manage to get so many Americans to sympathize and agree with them? Who are they, really? And why is it they have so much power, including the power to get someone fired simply for disagreeing with them? These are all questions that are worth asking and deserve answers, answers that you will not get from the major news networks (CNN, MSNBC, NBC, ABC, CBS, ESPN News, Vox, Slate, Media Matters, to name a few) or any politician, all of whom seems to have caved to this radical movement. The only network that somewhat reports the truth about BLM is Fox News, but even they are afraid to truly investigate them, with only Tucker Carlson and Laura Ingram being the ones to really challenge them on occasion.

The real truth is that BLM is not for racial justice but is for racial injustice. Their goal is to use violence and intimidation to overthrow the United States government and implement their own form of government based on Marxism, where whites are turned into second class citizens, if not outright eliminated; the local police departments no longer exist with them acting as police instead; and where individual freedom is a distant memory because everything will be about the collective, except if the collective doesn't like you they will eliminate you. All you have to do is listen to their chants and watch as they vandalize and loot businesses, smash cop cars, and physically assault anyone who gets in their way. They are not peaceful protestors. They are revolutionaries. They literally burn, loot, and murder.

If you wish to know the truth about this group and what it means for America, keep reading. If you prefer ignorance, by all means, throw this book out and enjoy your servitude.

# Where Did They Come From?

*"When those prominent in the status quo turn and label you an 'agitator' they are completely correct, for that is, in one word, your function—to agitate to the point of conflict." –Saul Alinsky, Rules for Radicals.*

Where did Black Lives Matter come from? They seem to have appeared out of nowhere, but for such a newly formed organization, they are very well-organized. According to Wikipedia, Black Lives Matter is

> *"...is an organized movement in the United States advocating for non-violent civil disobedience in protest against incidents of police brutality against African-American people.[2] An organization known simply as Black Lives Matter[a] exists as a decentralized network with about 16 chapters in the United States and Canada, while a larg-*

1

*er Black Lives Matter movement exists con-
sisting of various separate like-minded organizations such as Dream Defenders and
Assata's Daughters. The broader movement
and its related organizations typically advocate against police violence towards black
people, as well as for various other policy
changes considered to be related to black
liberation."[1]*

So, where did they come from?

They first appeared in 2013, after George Zimmerman
was acquitted for shooting and killing a black teenager named
Trayvon Martin, an incident that garnered the attention of
Barack Obama who said that if he had a son, he would look
like Trayvon. It started with a hashtag on Twitter: #Black-
LivesMatter, which quickly gained a following as everyone
who wanted to be trendy and show how conscious they were
of social justice retweeted it. But no one really thought about
the tweet itself.

In 2014, when Michael Brown was shot and killed by officer Darren Wilson, the media hyped it up as proof of police
brutality against black people, especially when the officer is
white, and once again, Black Lives Matter showed up with
a set of new tweets and the slogan "hands up, don't shoot".
Now, not only did Brown never say those words, but he was
not some innocent person either. The man had shoplifted before he was stopped by a police officer. The convenient store's
security camera shows this. However, this is not why he was
stopped. He was walking with a friend but was walking in
the middle of the street, which is why Officer Wilson stopped

Brown in the first place, and simply told him and his friend to get on the sidewalk. This was merely done for his safety, but Brown didn't see it that way. Instead of just saying, "thanks, man" and getting on the sidewalk, he chose to challenge the officer and a serious of shouts and cussing followed. As usually happens when people show an attitude towards a cop, the situation escalated. Witnesses say that Brown attacked Officer Wilson and tried to get his gun. A scuffle ensued and the gun went off with Brown being shot and killed. However, there are conflicting witness reports: some saying that Brown had his hands up when he was shot, and others saying that that was not the case and that Brown had, in fact, attacked the officer. It should be noted that Officer Wilson did shoot Brown six times, which adds fuel to the racial fire that stemmed from this incident. [2]

Now, could things have been handled differently? Of course, they could have! The whole situation got completely out of hand. No one is arguing that. Hindsight is always 20/20, but was Brown some innocent little boy that was hunted and then gunned down by a racist white cop as BLM and the media portrayed? No. The likelihood that race had anything to do with this is very nil. Does this incident justify what happened next in Ferguson? Absolutely not.

This is when Black Lives Matter, or BLM as they will be referred to from now on, was officially born. Soon after, they showed up with signs, protesting the death of Michael Brown, but what should have been a peaceful protest, turned into full-blown riots that overtook Ferguson, Missouri, leaving businesses destroyed and livelihoods ruined. The riots lasted for weeks with people vandalizing businesses, looting businesses, brawling in the streets, and attacking police. The riots spilled over into cities, such as, New York City and Los Angeles. Soon, the internet was ablaze with hashtags about black lives matter, and protestors organized online, demanding that there be an end to systemic racism, never mind the fact that no one could define it; an end to rampant police brutality towards minorities, even though there is no proof to back it up; and soon, they had their own manifesto published. They attracted the attention of the national media with news pundits all too willing to call them peaceful protestors who are just trying to correct grievances suffered by decades of racial inequality, and even then-president Barack Obama supported them. Soon, the streets were filled with BLM activists chanting, "Pigs in a blanket, fry like bacon!"[3] They had a mass following almost instantaneously, almost as though they were already organized and just waiting for the right moment.

Sound familiar?

Fast forward to 2020.

A man named George Floyd is killed when a white cop kneels on his neck, for nine minutes, allowing himself to be filmed, almost like he was posing for the camera, while other officers just stood around, not even trying to block the one camera that filmed the incident. In an era where everyone carries a camera in their pocket, only one person filmed it? The timing couldn't have been more perfect. 2020 is an election year. We're in the middle of a pandemic with people on lock down and filled with fear over the possibility of catching a virus. Shortages in the stores had become common, especially in certain areas. At the time George Floyd's name hit the airwaves, the country was ripe for anything to cause the pressure cooker to explode. After the video went viral, it didn't take long for BLM activists to show up with Antifa activists and start terrorizing, not just the city of Minneapolis, but almost every major city across the U.S, and they had far greater numbers than they did six years before. And while the media continues to call them peaceful protestors fighting racial injustice, BLM activists have joined forces with Antifa activists to burn cities, destroy businesses, loot businesses, attack cops, attack anyone who disagrees with them, and push a political agenda that will mean the end of not just law and order, but the United States as well.

Don't be fooled by their calls for racial justice, which is just a euphemism for black supremacy. BLM is a political movement that is nothing more than the continuation of the Black Liberation Movement, with a platform and an end goal. They are a political movement that was spawned out of chaos, thrives on chaos, and uses chaos to divide and conquer.

So, now that you know where they came from, or what gave rise to their movement, who are they, really?

# The Creators

*Give me your four-year-olds, and in a generation I
will build a socialist state.* —*Vladimir Lenin*

BLM was founded by admitted Marxists and career activists who are part of other groups that promote an end to the police, racial justice, environmental justice, and global justice—all of which are euphemisms for enacting government regulations that control the way in which you live. BLM wants you to believe that it is a grassroots movement, and the media does everything it can to facilitate this view, but it is anything but that. To understand what BLM is, you need to look at its founders: Patrisse Khan-Cullors, Alicia Garza, and Opal Tometi. Each of these women are activists for racial justice, which is a phrase that really means doing what is necessary to tear down western civilization and its past, undoing anything it created, and forcing modern whites to pay reparations for sins they never committed. They use the phrase justice, but it is not justice they seek but dominance over others, a common tactic among Marxists.

Let's consider each individual founder.

Patrisse Khan-Cullors is an admitted Marxist. In a video, she said, "We actually do have an ideological frame… we are trained Marxists."[4] She is a career activist and a self-described organizer and freedom-fighter. These descriptions may seem innocuous, but they aren't. They are chosen for a reason. No one wants to go against a freedom-fighter, but consider the history of every self-proclaimed freedom-fighter; they are all socialists. The Bolsheviks were freedom -fighters who supposedly fought to free the Russian people from the Czar's rule, but what they gave the Russian people was decades of tyranny, totalitarianism, and oppression where millions died and neighbor turned against neighbor. The revolutionaries during the French Revolution were freedom-fighters, yet their revolution quickly devolved into a literal reign of terror where people literally lost their heads, until Robespierre himself was beheaded by Madam Guillotine, creating the mother of all ironies, since he created the guillotine. Che Guevara was a self-described freedom-fighter, yet he executed any who disagreed with him, detested dissonance, executed homosexuals, and instituted his own reign of terror. Moral of the story: watch out for the self-proclaimed freedom fighters because it is not your freedom they are fighting for; it is control over you that they desire.

But I digress. Patrisse trained under known Marxist and former domestic terrorist Eric Mann who was part of the Weather Underground and Students for a Democratic Society, both of which were far left groups founded upon the principles of communism, and the Weather Underground was responsible for several domestic bombings, including one on the U.S. Capitol Building. In 2015 during an interview on Real News Network with Jared Bell, she praised Mann and admitted that the entire point of BLM'[5]s existence is to overthrow American capitalism and replace it with Marxist totalitarianism.

Patrisse supports far left causes, such as defunding the police, which New York has proven leave poor neighborhood defenseless against criminals and crime shot up at an exponential rate, resulting in rampant murder, rape, and theft. She is the founder of a group called Dignity and Power Now and a co-founder of Reform LA Jails now[6], which is a group built upon the belief that too many of the incarcerated are black or brown, therefore the jail system is racist. Their solution: stop arresting black and brown people. Never mind the fact that blacks commit the majority of the crimes in this country even though they make up less than half of the population. Dignity and Power Now is another leftist organization that and was founded in 2012, just two years before BLM, and promotes only people of color; it's very antiwhite.

Besides the groups she has helped form, which are also rooted in Marxism, Patrisse herself, in a video, admitted that she is a trained Marxist. She is a well-known organizer and activist and has had no other career, and is well-versed in the tactics of Marxists, one of which is forming groups that claim to stand against a particular injustice, doesn't matter if the injustice exists or not, and that, through them, you will achieve freedom. They drum up hatred towards other groups of people, in this case against whites and any one who promotes Americanism or capitalism, and capitalize on that division to achieve their end goal: complete control of the country and of you.

The other two founders are no different. Alicia Garza

describes herself as a proud queer, black woman, as though being queer or black should have anything to do with anything when fighting real injustice. You see, superficiality is everything to people like her. They don't care about character, just outward appearances. Alicia is another trained organizer and activist and has been one most of her life. She is the Special Projects Director for the National Domestic Workers Alliance that was founded in 2007. It was inspired by the National Domestic Workers Union for America, created in the 1960s by Dorothy Lee Bolden[7] and was an organization designed to help domestic workers, many of whom were women, to achieve fair pay, fair hours, and be able to negotiate better contracts.[8]

This organization ended in the 1990s[9] but found rebirth in the National Domestic Workers Alliance that claims to proudly carry on Bolden's work and even have an organization called We Dream in Black, which "aims to strengthen and expand the power and voices of Black domestic workers and amplify their contributions to a healthy multiracial and economically just society for all".[10] Again, it seems innocent enough, but notice how it only focuses on the rights of one group of people after instilling in your mind that they are a victim that needs rescuing. This is straight out Saul Alinsky's *Rules for* Radicals. The NDWA also promotes what they call a National Domestic Workers Bill of Rights which is supported by Democrat Senator Kamala Harris from California and Democrat Representative Pramil Jayapal from Washington state[11], two very far left members of Congress.

Alicia is no stranger to activism. She is part of other activist groups that are connected to or associated with even more activist groups, such as IPS, a group of progressives that promote progressive causes, all of which focus on movements meant to divide people and designed to make you feel as though you are a victim and that you need them to overcome your victimhood. Most of her writings and speeches center on how the police are inherently racist, how there is a lack of diversity within the entertainment industry, and is a big proponent of identity politics, which is little more than an us versus them ideology. According to her, the only way to truly understand the violence Black Americans face, people must "view this epidemic through a lens of race, gender, sexual orientation and gender identity".[12] Again, this sort of thing is straight out of Saul Alinsky's *Rules for Radicals*: divide and conquer. Your Marxists depend heavily on identity politics in order to divide people. There is always a victim and an oppressor. In this case, blacks are the victim and America, the police, and whites are viewed as the oppressors. This is what Alicia promotes. This will be her legacy.

The third co-founder of BLM is Opal Tometi. She is the daughter of Nigerian immigrants and has been an activist her whole life. Are you noticing a pattern? The founders are all professional activists. They have had no other career. Opal is also associated with BASI, another far left group that advocates for racial justice. Again, racial justice does not mean actual justice. Racial justice really means for every white person that is hired, a black person must also be hired, qualifications be damned. Racial justice can also mean that there should be more blacks in an area than whites. If there is an all white neighborhood, that is viewed as a place that practices racial injustice, but if there is an all black neighborhood, that is viewed as racially just. Racial justice is not about ensuring that there is equal opportunity for all, regardless of skin color; it's about promoting blacks, sometimes brown, and only black and brown to the exclusion of other races. This is what Opal promotes, but it goes much deeper than that.

Opal is a self-described student of liberation theology which is a pro-communist belief system that comes from the Black Liberation Movement. The Black Liberation movement is anti-capitalist, anti-imperialist, anti-freedom, anti-white, and promotes black supremacy. It's sole intention is to put blacks in position of power and to promote systems of black power by any means necessary.[13]

Opal has no qualms about hanging out with socialist dictators and even visited Nicolas Maduro of Venezuela, the socialist dictator of Venezuela that turned Venezuela from a prosperous, capitalist society in a socialist nightmare of totalitarianism, destitution, rampant poverty, and despair. Under Madura, Venezuela went from a first world paradise to a third world hell hole where people are unable to get basic amenities like reliable electricity, running water, and food. People are starving so badly in Venezuela that they resorted to eating their pets. This is who Opal admires. She visited him back in 2015 and took a picture with him, raising her fist in the typical black power salute.[14] She even got to observe a legislative election, which was a sham election, and praised the socialist dictator for his contributions to Venezuela. He destroyed his own country and this woman see nothing wrong with that. What do you think she will do to America if she gets what she wants? This woman is a long-time activist who promotes the destruction of America and capitalism.

All of three of them work for other organizations which are little more than front groups for Freedom Road Socialist Organization (FRSO), which is one of the largest radical left organizations in the United States. There are three other far left groups that actively promote Marxism in the U.S.: the Communist Party USA (CPUSA), Committees of Correspondence for Democracy and Socialism (CCDS), and the Democratic Socialists of America (DSA). The FRSO is descended directly from the New Communist Movement which heavily influence Mao Zedong. It split into two in 1999, forming the "FRSO/Fight Back and FRSO/OSCL (Freedom Road Socialist Organization/Organizaci?n Socialista del Camino para la Libertad)" [15] and is now comprised of dozens of groups. The founders of BLM are associated with FRSO/OSCL.

Do not be fooled by the sweet, innocent personas of these women. They are well-organized and well-trained soldiers in the Marxist ideology, in all of its forms. They are not promoting any sort of racial equality, i.e. equality under the law and equal opportunity; they are promoting the destruction of our culture, the destruction of our institutions, the destruction of our belief in individual liberty, and the destruction of real racial equality.

# Rooted in Marxism

*"Youth should learn to think and act as a mass. It is criminal to think as individuals!"—Che Guevara*

BLM's very foundation is in Marxism. Now, to be clear, I will be using the words communism, Marxism, social-ism, fascism, and progressivism interchangeably because there is little difference between them—they all stem from the ideology of Karl Marx. All of them believe that capitalism is evil and needs to be destroyed. They all believe in ushering in a revolution through violent means to destroy the institutions of your country so as to usher in the new society rooted in Marxism. They all believe in pitting people against each other by dividing them into groups where some are the oppressors and others are the oppressed. They all believe in using violence to shut down dissenters. Individual freedom is not one of their concepts. They all have the same end: a society that devolves into a police state where there is no freedom, your life is dictated to you by the state, and any criticism is met with brute force. All of these tactics BLM practices.

The founders of BLM are trained Marxists and have admitted as much. Their own site literally copies the Communist Manifesto. Look at this 2020 initiative of theirs.

*"BLM's #WhatMatters2020 is a campaign aimed to maximize the impact of the BLM movement by galvanizing BLM supporters and allies to the polls in the 2020 U.S Presidential Election to build collective power and ensure candidates are held accountable for the issues that systematically and disproportionately impact Black and under-served communities across the nation.*

*"BLM's #WhatMatters2020 will focus on issues concerning racial injustice, police brutality, criminal justice reform, Black immigration, economic injustice, LGBTQIA+ and human rights, environmental injustice, access to healthcare, access to quality education, and voting rights and suppression."*[16]

Notice the focus on "collective power". This is a Marxist concept. There is no individuality in communism, only collectivism and only the collective is important. At the same time, they want to focus on environmental justice, economic justice, immigration, and the LGBT movement. What do all of these have to do with two black men being shot and killed by police? Absolutely nothing, because this movement is not about stopping police brutality towards blacks, especially when you consider there really is no rampant police brutality towards blacks, or any group. Let's put it this way: it's not as rampant as they make it seem. Not that there are not incidences here and there, but it is not everywhere or happening all the time. Consider the graph from Statista. For the year 2020, as of July 18, only 105 blacks (out of 40.2 million[17], making it 0.00026%) have been fatally shot by an officer. But look at the numbers for whites, it's double. Though, to put it in perspective, there have been 204 whites out of 197 million[18], or 0.00010%, have been fatally shot. The numbers are comparable, and keep in mind that for the past six to eight weeks there have been riots in major cities across the

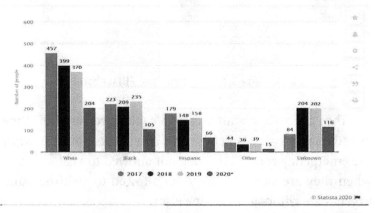

Police butality statistics for the last four years. Taken from Statista.

U.S., leading to increased altercations between people and the police.

But hyping up people's emotions over one or two incidents makes a great way to gather followers and use them so as to implement the change you want.

2018 Crime Statistics from the FBI website.

They claim they want access to healthcare, but don't they already have access to healthcare? Are blacks not allowed in the emergency room? Are they not allowed to visit a doctor when they are sick? Are they not allowed to visit the same urgent care clinics as everyone else?

They want equal access to education, but do blacks not already have such access? Are there no public schools? Are there no libraries? Do they not have the internet, and if they can't afford it, are there no coffee shops where you can access the free WIFI? Are there no bookstores where they can go in and read a book or two and then put it back on the shelf? Not that I'm saying you should do that in a bookstore, but some do. Most people, no matter their skin color, have smart phones which are connected to a network, giving them access to terabytes of information. Are they not able to go to the same colleges as everyone else? Are they unable to get funding through grants, student loans, or even by joining the military? The truth is there are a lot of scholarships designed specifically for black people and no one else that will give them funding to go to a college of their choice. A simple Google® search brings up a list of at least 70 such scholarships. So, they are not being denied access to education. If anything, our modern world with the internet has made it easier to get an education, but here is the other half of the coin: your education depends upon you. You have to value it; you have to want to be educated; and you have to take the time and put in the effort to acquire an education. You cannot depend upon anyone to do it for you. You cannot depend upon the schools to teach you everything you need to know. They are good place to get started, but most of what you learn will be outside of school.

The problem is not that blacks don't have access to an education. The problem is that, like so many in this country, they don't value it. Too many people in America, no matter their skin color, see little value in being literate, knowing their history, knowing basic math, knowing basic science, and in having common sense. BLM knows this, but they don't care, because they do not want blacks, or any of their followers, to be educated. People who are educated, know their history and do not have a political axe to grind, see BLM for what they are: a Marxist pimp that whores out their followers to do their dirty work and make them money. If BLM really wanted to ensure the black community was educated, they would teach their youth the value of getting a real education, the value in knowing how to read above an elementary level, the value in knowing history even if it offends them, and the value in critical thinking. And I'm not saying that the black community is unique in not caring about getting an education; this is something that plagues America as a whole, where students study for the test and then forget everything they were taught, choosing to worry about the latest trend on social media instead. But what I am saying is that BLM could impart on people the importance of being educated, and help change people's perceptions about education, but they don't do that. Instead, they choose to make people believe that they are oppressed and that that oppression is due to inherent, systemic racism, even though, anyone can go to school.

Making people feel as though they are oppressed is a common tactic among Marxists. They need their followers to feel wronged. They need that anger, that unbridled and uncontrolled anger so that they can use it for their ends.

But let's look at their manifesto and their demands. It interesting how every activist group has some sort of manifesto, which mirrors Marx's own manifesto and the demands of every socialist that has ever walked the earth.

> "We see ourselves as part of the **global Black family** [emphasis added], and we are aware of the different ways we are impacted or privileged as Black people who exist in different parts of the world."[19]

The thing about Marxists is everything is about the collective and BLM is no different. This focus on a global family focuses on being part of a group. Again, there is no individuality allowed under Marxism, in all of its forms. But this focus on a global family should also tell you that this is a global movement, not grassroots. It also means that BLM has been around for a while and that the founders were busy making all of the right connections before officially launching a brand new activist group that would focus on tearing people apart as they try to dismantle the United States.

> *"We are guided by the fact that all Black lives matter, regardless of actual or perceived sexual identity, gender identity, gender expression, economic status, ability, disability, religious beliefs or disbeliefs, immigration status, or location."*[20]

Notice how they are being very inclusive in that they have opened the door for other activist groups such as the LGBT movement, which also has Marxist ties, and for organizations, such as, Open Society, which advocates open borders, which would effectively destroy the country.

> *"We are self-reflexive and do the work required to dismantle cisgender privilege and uplift Black trans folk, especially Black trans women who continue to be disproportionately impacted by trans-antagonistic violence."*[21]

Once again, BLM's manifesto seems to be about more

than just promoting black lives. They are trying to squeeze everything in there so that they can coordinate and gain support from other Marxist groups, but it also shows that BLM is concerned with something more broad. It talks about cisgender privilege as a way to give their followers another cause to fight for. There is no such thing as cisgender privilege and the word cisgender itself is only two or three years old and was quickly adopted by those on the left, especially the transgender movement, as a way of rallying their base and garnering sympathy. Marx did something similar. In his Communist Manifesto, he did more than just talk about the abuses the proletariat suffered under the bourgeoisie. He wanted his readers to believe that the bourgeoisie was privileged and discriminatory against any who was not like them. Basically, Marx wanted to generate envy and hatred towards the wealthy, and this is what BLM is doing here: generating hatred and envy towards anyone who is heterosexual, and white.

> "We disrupt the Western-prescribed nuclear family structure requirement by supporting each other as extended families and "villages" that collectively care for one another, especially our children, to the degree that mothers, parents, and children are comfortable."[22]

Yes, they want to eradicate the nuclear family, that means, families where there is both a mother and a father, and basically take away parental rights. Your kids are not your kids, according to BLM. They want "extended families" or "villages"—remember Hillary Clinton's "it takes a village" campaign—to raise your children and "collectively care" for them. Such a notion puts children under the control of the state where the state will raise them and raise them to be perfect little communists who will do the bidding of the elites in charge. Karl Marx also thought that children should be raised by the state and that the nuclear family should be abolished because the family, parents who raise their children, are a threat to the communist state.

In addition to their manifesto, BLM has a list of demands, which they have released since the death of George Floyd. As you read them, they should seem familiar; they are the Democrat Party Platform, Antifa's platform, The Socialist Party USA platform, and were also the platform of the Nazis, the Bolsheviks, Mao Zedong, the Cuban Revolutionaries of the 1960s, and the radical Marxist groups that plagued the U.S. during the 1960s. This is their agenda:

They want an end to all jails, prisons, and detention facilities, meaning that they want them closed and all construction on future facilities to end. They want black criminals arrested for prostitution or drug related offenses to be released and their records expunged and for the War on Drugs to end.[23]

They want to eradicate the police by defunding it and eliminating it all together. In the words of Alexandria Ocasio-Cortez, "Defund the police means defund the police."[24]

They want to abolish ICE, all immigration detention centers, and the Border Patrol.

They want to legalize prostitution, universal healthcare, and reparations.

They want the U.S. government to pass Bill H.R.40, the "Commission to Study Reparation Proposals for African-Americans Act", which would give reparations to blacks. These reparations will come in the form of free education up through the college level for all blacks, including ones in prison and illegal immigrants, in addition to their student loans being forgiven and "support for lifetime learning programs".[25] These reparations are to also come in the form of a guaranteed universal income for blacks, and only blacks. They want reparations for

> *"cultural and educational exploitation, erasure, and extraction of our communities in the form of mandated public school curriculums that critically examine the political, economic, and social impacts of colonialism and slavery, and funding to support, build, preserve, and restore cultural assets and sacred sites to ensure the recognition and honoring of our collective struggles and triumphs."[26]*

Never mind the fact that these same people are trying to erase American history and its culture.

They demand economic justice and under that plan all wealth would be redistributed and the tax code would be rewritten to radically redistribute wealth on the federal, state, and local levels. This plan would include more unionization of workers in what are termed "on demand" jobs. They want all trade agreement renegotiated to benefit the workers. In addition to the redistribution of wealth, they want

> *"tax incentives, loans and other government*

*directed resources, support the development of cooperative or social economy networks to help facilitate trade across and in Black communities globally. All aid in the form of grants, loans or contracts to help facilitate this must go to Black led or Black supported networks and organizations as defined by the communities.*[27]

BLM wants resources to be collectively owned and distributed as described below.

*"A right to restored land, clean air, clean water and housing and an end to the exploitative privatization of natural resources — including land and water. We seek democratic control over how resources are preserved, used and distributed and do so while honoring and respecting the rights of our Indigenous family."*[2829]

Basically, the above advocates an end to private property, but are also taking it one step further by wanting to give what they see as stolen land back to the American Indians. And, yes, I said American Indians. They are not Native Americans because America did not exist at that time; it wasn't even an idea, and they migrated to the continent from somewhere else, and I am not giving in to this politically correct bullshit.

BLM refers to "democratic control" of natural resources, but there will be nothing democratic about it; it will be controlled by the government. This is something Karl Marx advocated for as he writes in his Communist Manifesto, "Abolition of property in land and application of all rents of land to public purposes" and an "abolition of all rights of inheritance".[30] Basically, all land will belong to the state, not the people and certainly not individuals. If you own a farm or a ranch, it will be taken from you by the power of the government if BLM, and those like them, get what they want. All factories, all businesses, all agricultural lands will be owned by the state, just like Karl Marx described in his manifesto, "Extension of factories and instruments of production owned by the State; the bringing into cultivation of waste-lands, and the improvement of the soil generally in accordance with a common plan."[31]

And in addition to all of this, BLM also wants:

> *"Financial support of Black alternative institutions including policy that subsidizes and offers low-interest, interest-free or federally guaranteed low-interest loans to promote the development of cooperatives (food, residential, etc.), land trusts and culturally responsive health infrastructures that serve the collective needs of our communities."[32]*

Basically, they are demanding black owned banks that will guarantee loans to blacks so that black communities will be funded and able to have their needs taken care of. But who do you think is really going to pay it? The government will with tax money they take from those who are viewed as having oppressed blacks, i.e. whites. The only way for this part of their manifesto to be accomplished is if the financial industry is centralized under the government, which is something Marx promoted, "Centralisation of credit in the hands of the state, by means of a national bank with State capital and an exclusive monopoly."[33]

In addition to economic and environmental justice, BLM wants universal, automatic voter registration and they want same day voter registration for all previously incarcerated people and illegal immigrants. That's right. BLM wants illegals to vote in U.S. elections.[34]

They also want the military to have its funding cut so that it can be redistributed to "domestic infrastructure and community well-being."[35]

And let's add no bail and no death penalty to all this.[36] This just scratches the surface of what they want. The follow pages list all of the demands of Black Live Matter in addition to the demands of Karl Marx's *Communist Manifesto*. It is almost word for word, except for BLM the proletariat are the blacks and the bourgeoisie are the whites.

The following is their manifesto as compared to Karl Marx's.

## Black Lives Matter

Every day, we recommit to healing ourselves and each other, and to co-creating alongside comrades, allies, and family a culture where each person feels seen, heard, and supported.

We acknowledge, respect, and celebrate differences and commonalities.

We work vigorously for freedom and justice for Black people and, by extension, all people.

We intentionally build and nurture a beloved community that is bonded together through a beautiful struggle that is restorative, not depleting.

We are unapologetically Black in our positioning. In affirming that Black Lives Matter, we need not qualify our position. To love and desire freedom and justice for ourselves is a prerequisite for wanting the same for others.

We see ourselves as part of the global Black family, and we are aware of the different ways we are impacted or privileged as Black people who exist in different parts of the world.

We are guided by the fact that all Black lives matter, regardless of actual or perceived sexual identity, gender identity, gender expression, economic status, ability, disability, religious beliefs or disbeliefs, immigration status, or location.

We make space for transgender brothers and sisters to participate and lead.

We are self-reflexive and do the work required to dismantle cisgender privilege and uplift Black trans folk, especially Black trans women who continue to be disproportionately impacted by trans-antagonistic violence.

We build a space that affirms Black women and is free from sexism, misogyny, and environments in which men are centered.

We practice empathy. We engage comrades with the intent to learn about and connect with their contexts.

We make our spaces family-friendly and enable parents to fully participate with their children. We dismantle the patriarchal practice that requires mothers to work "double shifts" so that they can mother in private even as they participate in public justice work.

We disrupt the Western-prescribed nuclear family structure requirement by supporting each other as extended families and "villages" that collectively care for one another, especially our children, to the degree that mothers, parents, and children are comfortable.

We foster a queer-affirming network. When we gather, we do so with the intention of freeing ourselves from the tight grip of heteronormative thinking, or rather, the belief that all in the world are heterosexual (unless s/he or they disclose otherwise).

We cultivate an intergenerational and communal network free from ageism. We believe that all people, regardless of age, show up with the capacity to lead and learn.

We embody and practice justice, liberation, and peace in our engagements with one another.

## Movement for Black Lives

Movement for Black Lives is an arm of Black Lives Matter.

### Reparations

We demand reparations for past and continuing harms. The

government, responsible corporations and other institutions that have profited off of the harm they have inflicted on Black people — from colonialism to slavery through food and housing redlining, mass incarceration, and surveillance — must repair the harm done. This includes:

1. Reparations for the systemic denial of access to high quality educational opportunities in the form of full and free access for all Black people (including undocumented and currently and formerly incarcerated people) to lifetime education including: free access and open admissions to public community colleges and universities, technical education (technology, trade and agricultural), educational support programs, retroactive forgiveness of student loans, and support for lifetime learning programs.

2. Reparations for the continued divestment from, discrimination toward and exploitation of our communities in the form of a guaranteed minimum livable income for all Black people, with clearly articulated corporate regulations.

3. Reparations for the wealth extracted from our communities through environmental racism, slavery, food apartheid, housing discrimination and racialized capitalism in the form of corporate and government reparations focused on healing ongoing physical and men-

tal trauma, and ensuring our access and control of food sources, housing and land.

4. Reparations for the cultural and educational exploitation, erasure, and extraction of our communities in the form of mandated public school curriculums that critically examine the political, economic, and social impacts of colonialism and slavery, and funding to support, build, preserve, and restore cultural assets and sacred sites to ensure the recognition and honoring of our collective struggles and triumphs.

5. Legislation at the federal and state level that requires the United States to acknowledge the lasting impacts of slavery, establish and execute a plan to address those impacts. This includes the immediate passage of H.R.40, the "Commission to Study Reparation Proposals for African-Americans Act" or subsequent versions which call for reparations remedies.

## Invest-Divest

We demand investments in the education, health and safety of Black people, instead of investments in the criminalizing, caging, and harming of Black people. We want investments in Black communities, determined by Black communities, and divestment from exploitative forces including prisons, fossil fuels, police, surveillance and exploitative corporations. This includes:

1. A reallocation of funds at the federal, state

and local level from policing and incarceration (JAG, COPS, VOCA) to long-term safety strategies such as education, local restorative justice services, and employment programs.

2. The retroactive decriminalization, immediate release and record expungement of all drug related offenses and prostitution, and reparations for the devastating impact of the "war on drugs" and criminalization of prostitution, including a reinvestment of the resulting savings and revenue into restorative services, mental health services, job programs and other programs supporting those impacted by the sex and drug trade.

3. Real, meaningful, and equitable universal health care that guarantees: proximity to nearby comprehensive health centers, culturally competent services for all people, specific services for queer, gender nonconforming, and trans people, full bodily autonomy, full reproductive services, mental health services, paid parental leave, and comprehensive quality child and elder care.

4. A constitutional right at the state and federal level to a fully-funded education which includes a clear articulation of the right to: a free education for all, special protections for queer and trans students, wrap around services, social workers, free health services (including reproductive body autonomy), a curriculum that acknowledges and addresses

students' material and cultural needs, physical activity and recreation, high quality food, free daycare, and freedom from unwarranted search, seizure or arrest.

5. A divestment from industrial multinational use of fossil fuels and investment in community- based sustainable energy solutions.

6. A cut in military expenditures and a reallocation of those funds to invest in domestic infrastructure and community well-being.

## Economic Justice

We demand economic justice for all and a reconstruction of the economy to ensure Black communities have collective ownership, not merely access. This includes:

1. A progressive restructuring of tax codes at the local, state, and federal levels to ensure a radical and sustainable redistribution of wealth.

2. Federal and state job programs that specifically target the most economically marginalized Black people, and compensation for those involved in the care economy. Job programs must provide a living wage and encourage support for local workers centers, unions, and Black-owned businesses which are accountable to the community.

3. A right to restored land, clean air, clean water and housing and an end to the exploitative privatization of natural resources — including land and water. We seek democratic con-

trol over how resources are preserved, used and distributed and do so while honoring and respecting the rights of our Indigenous family.

4. The right for workers to organize in public and private sectors especially in "On Demand Economy" jobs.

5. Restore the Glass-Steagall Act to break up the large banks, and call for the National Credit Union Administration and the US Department of the Treasury to change policies and practices around regulation, reporting and consolidation to allow for the continuation and creation of black banks, small and community development credit unions, insurance companies and other financial institutions.

6. n end to the Trans-Pacific Partnership and a renegotiation of all trade agreements to prioritize the interests of workers and communities.

7. Through tax incentives, loans and other government directed resources, support the development of cooperative or social economy networks to help facilitate trade across and in Black communities globally. All aid in the form of grants, loans or contracts to help facilitate this must go to Black led or Black supported networks and organizations as defined by the communities.

8. Financial support of Black alternative institutions including policy that subsidizes and

offers low-interest, interest-free or federally guaranteed low-interest loans to promote the development of cooperatives (food, residential, etc.), land trusts and culturally responsive health infrastructures that serve the collective needs of our communities.

9. Protections for workers in industries that are not appropriately regulated including domestic workers, farm workers, and tipped workers, and for workers — many of whom are Black women and incarcerated people—who have been exploited and remain unprotected. This includes the immediate passage at the Federal and state level of the Domestic Workers Bill of Rights and extension of worker protections to incarcerated people.

## Community Control

We demand a world where those most impacted in our communities control the laws, institutions, and policies that are meant to serve us – from our schools to our local budgets, economies, police departments, and our land – while recognizing that the rights and histories of our Indigenous family must also be respected. This includes:

1. Direct democratic community control of local, state, and federal law enforcement agencies, ensuring that communities most harmed by destructive policing have the power to hire and fire officers, determine disciplinary ac-

tion, control budgets and policies, and sub-
poena relevant agency information.

2.  An end to the privatization of education and
    real community control by parents, students
    and community members of schools includ-
    ing democratic school boards and commu-
    nity control of curriculum, hiring, firing and
    discipline policies.
3.  Participatory budgeting at the local, state and
    federal level.

**Political Power**

We demand independent Black political power and Black
self-determination in all areas of society. We envision a remaking of the current U.S. political system in order to create a real
democracy where Black people and all marginalized people
can effectively exercise full political power. This includes:

1.  An end to the criminalization of Black polit-
    ical activity including the immediate release
    of all political prisoners and an end to the re-
    pression of political parties.
2.  Public financing of elections and the end
    of money controlling politics through end-
    ing super PACs and unchecked corporate
    donations.
3.  Election protection, electoral expansion and
    the right to vote for all people including: full
    access, guarantees, and protections of the
    right to vote for all people through universal

voter registration, automatic voter registration, pre-registration for 16-year-olds, same day voter registration, voting day holidays, Online Voter Registration (OVR), enfranchisement of formerly and presently incarcerated people, local and state resident voting for undocumented people, and a ban on any disenfranchisement laws.

4. Full access to technology including net neutrality and universal access to the internet without discrimination and full representation for all.

5. Protection and increased funding for Black institutions including Historically Black Colleges and Universities (HBCU's), Black media and cultural, political and social formations.

## Respect Protestors

Basically, BLM wants to be allowed to do whatever they want, which is burn property, vandalize property, and steel property without an consequences, hence the following demands. That is like a burglar breaking into your home, stealing you stuff while demanding that you not press charges or have them prosecuted for breaking into your home and stealing your possessions. This is Black Lives Matter. Like the Communists of old, they want to be able to do whatever they want and even demand that we just let them act like thugs and criminals, but don't you dare steal from them or stand up to them, because they will not be merciful.

We demand that the rights of protestors be respected and protected and that there be no abuse of powers. We Demand:

1. Violations of property should never be equated with the violation of human life.
2. That local and state officials ensure that there are no abuse of powers
3. No use of lethal force on protestors.

All of these demands come from either the Black Lives Matter website, or the Movement for Black Lives', which is a subsidiary of Black Live Matter, website.

**The Communist Manifesto:**

1. Abolition of property in land and application of all rents of land to public purposes.

2. A heavy progressive or graduated income tax.

3. Abolition of all rights of inheritance.

4. Confiscation of the property of all emigrants and rebels.

5. Centralisation of credit in the hands of the state, by means of a national bank with State capital and an exclusive monopoly.

6. Centralisation of the means of communication and transport in the hands of the State.

7. Extension of factories and instruments of production

owned by the State; the bringing into cultivation of waste-lands, and the improvement of the soil generally in accordance with a common plan.

8. Equal liability of all to work. Establishment of industrial armies, especially for agriculture.

9. Combination of agriculture with manufacturing industries; gradual abolition of all the distinction between town and country by a more equable distribution of the populace over the country.

10. Free education for all children in public schools. Abolition of children's factory labour in its present form. Combination of education with industrial production, &c, &c.

# Not the First

*"We have no compassion and we ask no compassion
from you. When our turn comes, we shall not make
excuses for the terror." —Karl Marx*

B LM and its subsidiaries are not the first to promote
such anti-American ideas, and, yes, Marxism in all
of its forms is anti-American. They are incompatible
with the U.S. Constitution and cannot coexist with a free society. Their roots are in communism and they are heavily
influenced by Black Liberation Theology. BLM is not the first
group to promote the idea that an entire group of people are
oppressed just to use them for a political agenda. BLM is just
continuing the Marxist revolution that was started over a
century ago. They are not the first to promote the dissolution
of individual liberty, nor will they be the last. In short, they
are just another tier of revolutionaries pretending to be freedom-fighters in a long history of people who spread violence
and oppression by claiming to combat both.

Consider the symbol they use: the fist raised high in the

air. Have any of their followers bothered to look up the history of that symbol? No, they haven't. The fist raised high in the air has been the symbol of the Bolsheviks, the followers of Mao Zedong, The Black Panther Party; the New Black Panther Party, the Weather Underground, the Socialist Party USA, the Cuban revolutionaries led by Fidel Castro, the revolutionaries led by Che Guevara, and the Black Liberation Movement. The LGBT movement and your transactivists also use the fist as a symbol of their movement, which should tell you something about them: like BLM, they are rooted in Marxism and want to overthrow America's capitalist society. The fist is not a symbol of pride or solidarity to a cause, it is a symbol of Marxist revolutionaries, the same revolutionaries who are responsible for the death of millions of people and the destruction of countries worldwide. Even the Nazis used a version of the fist in the air as their symbol; Hitler just changed it slightly so that his movement would stand out against the others that were raging across Germany after World War 1.

BLM and their founders know exactly what they are doing. They are following the blueprint of those who came before them.

## The Bolsheviks

The Bolsheviks were revolutionaries led by Vladimir Lenin, who was a follower of Marxist ideology and an admitted communist. He is even quoted as saying that the goal of socialism is communism. The peasantry of Russia at the time suffered miserably under Czar Nikolas, and it didn't take much for Lenin to use those emotions to work them up into a mob. They used violence and intimidation to overthrow the

Russian monarchy, murdered the Czar and his family, and brought their own reign of terror as they implemented their communist dream, or I should say, nightmare.

## The Nazis

I know what you are thinking, "The Nazis were fascists! There is a difference!"

In reality, there is little difference between communism, socialism, or fascism. The Nazis called themselves the National Socialist German Worker's Party. Notice how all of your collective groups claim to be for the worker, or the oppressed? The Nazis were socialists, or communists, there is little difference between the two, but they took it a step further and added their own spin to it. Hitler was a believer in communism and enamored by the communists in Germany at the time, but the communists didn't hate the Jews. The communists were focused on painting the wealthy as the bad guys, whereas Hitler, loathed and despised the Jews. He also wanted to be the one in charge, and that wasn't going to happen if he joined the communist party, so he basically formed his own, but the ideas he espoused were rooted in Marxism, and he used the same colors on his flag.

The Nazis used violence as a tool to gain power in Germany, destroying businesses and looting them and physically attacking anyone who stood against them. Dissent was not allowed and met with force. Like the Bolsheviks, the Nazis used violence and intimidation to gain power, until they managed to take over all of Germany. And when they succeeded, Hitler nationalized all in industry in Germany, but he was more clever about it; he did it in such a way where individual thought they owned their businesses, but if they didn't produce what Germany wanted, it was taken from them. [37]

## The Cultural Revolutionaries under Mao Zedong

Mao was an admitted communist. His cultural revolution consisted of tearing down statues and all remnants of the past, so as to erase Chinese history during his take over of China. His followers were rabid in their approach and utilized violence to achieve their ends, destroying business, taking over private property, burning as they went, and executing any who stood against them in the streets. The goal of Mao's cultural revolution was to eliminate all evidence of China having ever been a capitalist society and to get rid of China's rich, pre-communist, history. Massacres took place across the country as the Red Guards helped seal Mao's hold on power, and it is believed that about 20 million people[38] were killed. Dissent was not tolerated. You either joined Mao's movement or died.

## The Black Panther Party

The Black Panther Party (BPP) was founded by Huey P. Newton and Bobby Seale in Oakland, California. Both were admitted Marxists and believed in black nationalism as well as using violence to achieve their ends.[39] They called it armed self-defense—funny how BLM says the same thing—but it was nothing more than anarchist actions meant to intimidate and scare the populace into accepting their political stance and movement. Any who dissented from them were met with physical violence by supporters. The goal of the BPP was to overthrow the U.S. government and implement a new one that would promote black people across the country as the superior race and whites would be subjugated beneath them.[40] The goal of the BPP was free housing and education for blacks and an end to police brutality. Sound familiar?

The BPP had a Ten Point Program that is eerily similar to BLM's manifesto and demands. It consisted of freedom and power for the black community, full employment for blacks, overthrowing capitalism because they believed it robbed the black community, decent housing, all black men to be exempt from military service, an end to police brutality towards blacks, blacks to be tried by other blacks, land, housing, education, justice, and peace.[41] On the surface it sounds innocent, but every communist, revolutionary movement asks for these same things, with the exception that the BPP brought race into the mix, choosing to separate people by race instead of by wealth with their calls for black power.

## The Black Liberation Movement

The Black Liberation Movement gave rise to the Black Liberation Army and Black Liberation Theology, which rose out of the Black Panther Party. The Black Liberation Movement used violence in its goal of ridding itself of what it viewed as an oppressive colonialist America. Being anti-colonialist or anti-imperialist is a core tenet of the followers of Marxism. The Black Liberation Army was a terrorist group that wanted to further black power and its members attacked the police across the country.[42]

Part of the Black Liberation Movement is Black Liberation Theology which promotes black nationalism, using a foundation of bitterness and victimhood—basically, it preached that blacks are always victims of racism—and promoted social justice. It promotes Marxist ideals, but wraps it in a religious cloak. Black Liberation Theology promoted the belief that God favors black people and agreed with Malcolm X's proclamation that whites are nothing more than white devils and are inherently racist.[43] Black Liberation Theology does not preach growing closer to God or trying to live humbly and live by the teachings of Chris because, according to them, that is a white man's religion and therefore oppressive; instead, Black Liberation Theology encourages blacks to think of themselves as victims, while talking about the struggle to escape white racism.

The goal of the Black Liberation Movement is to spread division, by using Black Liberation Theology to do so. It promotes the idea of victimization, just like Marxism, and all of its offshoots, does because it needs people to believe they are victimized in order to survive. In the case of Black Liberation Theology, they promote the idea that blacks are victims of a white supremacist society and that blacks will always be victims in America and that the only way to thrive is to segregate themselves and to not think of themselves as Americans, but to think of themselves as black warriors for justice. This is similar to Marxism where it promoted the idea that if you are not wealthy, you are a victim of the wealthy class and will always be exploited by them until you rise up and overthrow your masters. Black Liberation Theology uses this as well.

It preaches that blacks are in poverty because of white oppression, while ignoring the fact that many in the black community drop out of school, choose to participate in crime, choose to murder one another (black on black crime affects the black community more than anything else, but is never addressed by groups such as BLM), and grow up in single family homes—all of which affect how well individuals will do in life. They don't care that Barack Obama, a black man, managed to become president of the United States and was elected twice. They don't care that there are black senators and representatives in Congress, or that there are black teachers, doctors, lawyers, business owners, contractors, IT professionals, to name a few. None of that matters to them. Black Liberation Theology preaches that blacks will always be victims and that nothing has changed in America because America is inherently racist, while ignoring the fact that America ended slavery, passed the Civil Rights Act of 1964 and 1968, passed affirmative action (which is basically reverse racism), and that there are a multitude of scholarships and grants to help blacks go to college; and though not perfect, America has made great strides in promoting equality and equal opportunity for blacks. But this doesn't matter to the Black Liberation Theologists and its followers because, according to them, blacks will always be victims of white oppression until white society is overthrown. If you're black and a white person accidentally bumps into you, according to BLM, all black power movements, and Black Liberation Theology, it was racism and you are now a victim of that racism. If you bring up any of the points mentioned above, your Black Liberation Theologists will say that you are just promoting white lies and accuse you of promoting systemic racism.

At its core, the Black Liberation Movement is a movement that promotes victimhood and violence, just like its influencer Karl Marx, except, for them, blacks are the oppressed and whites, especially pro-American whites, are the oppressors and they intend to overthrow their oppressors by any means necessary. They preach marginalization because they need black people to always believe they are marginalized, no matter how well their life is, because that is how they gain power over them and remain in power.[44] This theology, this movement, heavily influences BLM because much of what BLM promotes, such as the idea that blacks are discriminated against at an exponential rate, comes directly from Black Liberation Theology and the movement it inspired.

## The Weather Underground

The Weather Underground was a terrorist organization from the 1970s and was also heavily influenced by and a promoter of Marxist ideology. It was formed in 1968 and was originally called the Weatherman, but eventually changed their name to The Weather Underground. They advocated armed resistance to what they viewed as an imperialist society, i.e. the United States and the United States government, by declaring war against the U.S., and wanted to "lead white kids into armed revolution". They bombed the Pentagon (May 19, 1972) and the U.S. Capitol building (March 1, 1971). On October 8, 1969 they staged a riot to protest the Vietnam War which became known as "Days of Rage"[45] which resulted in damaged property and cops and rioters being injured.[46]

As with most violent groups like this, it was formed by college students who saw the decade following WWII, the 1950s, as a time of oppression for blacks and a time of "complacency, stagnation, and authoritarianism", despite the fact that it was actually a time of prosperity and peace, though, in certain areas of the country, segregation separated whites and blacks and blacks were discriminated against. But this is the problem when children are raised in times of peace, they seem to hate it and thirst for something that will allow them to make their mark on the world, making it easy for them to become radicalized, which is the case of the Weather Underground, but they went beyond being radicalized;

they chose violence as a means to an end, and that was to destroy the very country that allowed them to live in peace and prosperity.

The Weather Underground ended up being an offshoot of Students for a Democratic Society (SDS) because it was too violent for them. SDS wanted to fight what they viewed as corporate greed and was "an amalgam of left-liberal, socialist, anarchist and increasingly Marxist currents and tendencies,"[47] from which the Weather Underground broke off from, choosing violence as a means to an end and became full-fledged communists. They detested capitalism and saw America as a great evil where white supremacy reigned supreme and adopted most of their ideas from the communist ideologies, social constructs, and doctrines of Cuba. The following best describes the roots of The Weather Underground.

> *"FBI documents reveal that an estimated 4,000 people tied to the 1960s movements visited Cuba for the purposes of learning how to best spark a full-scale revolution in America. Those people included academics, members of the New Left, and even violent activists bent on change. And a small number of them (about 30) were Weathermen, who met directly with Vietnamese revolutionaries in 1969, and whose 'philosophy was an incendiary — some would say infantile — mix of Marx, Ché Guevara and Ho Chi Minh, lubricated by free love [...] LSD and daddy's cash,' according to The Guardian."*[48]

For over a decade, The Weather Underground embarked on a reign of terror, instigating 25 bombings, and though no one died in these bombings, only because they gave some warning before the bomb went off, resulting to murder was never far off for them. There was an instance where one member said that no one died, referring to the U.S. Capitol building bombing, because they weren't ready to go that far yet, basically implying that if they continued to not get what they wanted, then they would escalate to murder. Two of their most famous leaders are Bill Ayers and Bernadine Dohrn. Ayers is a professor at the University of Illinois Chicago and has lamented that the group never went far enough, and Dohrn is a retired associate professor from Northwestern University's Children and Justice Center and mentored one of BLM's founders. [49] In a way, BLM is a continuation of The Weather Underground in addition to being a continuation of the Black Liberation Movement.

## The New Black Panther Party

The New Black Panther Party (NBPP) dresses like the Black Panthers, and are a militant black nationalist group, adopting the militaristic uniforms of the black panthers, but are not officially affiliated with the Black Panthers, who have denounced the group. However, the NBPP ideology is rooted in Black Liberation Theology and describe themselves as revolutionaries whose goal is the "Black/Afrikan People's liberation struggle, and to mobilize the masses towards self-determination."[50] Violence is a part of their creed as it seems to follow them wherever they go.

This is just a short list of other radical groups that have come before and from which BLM has modeled their organization and tactics from. Do not be fooled. BLM is not a grass-roots movement. It never was. It is well funded and well-organized and its goal is to continue and complete the work of the above-mentioned groups. The goal of your Marxists, communists, Nazis, counter culture revolutionaries, and the Black Liberation Army has always been to eradicate capitalism, eradicate individuality and individual freedom, and to force the world to live under their rules.

# Islamic Terrorist Ties

*"I am sure that the Japanese, the Chinese and the peoples of Islam will always be closer to us than, for example, France, in spite of the fact that we are related by blood (...)"* —Adolf Hitler

D on't roll your eyes at this. No one in the mainstream media wants to report on this, but the truth is, BLM has ties to Islamic terrorist groups. And, no, I don't mean radical Islam; I mean Islam because when you study the religion, the Koran, and the life of Mohammed, you will realize that, in the words of Brigit Gabriel, Islam is radical and determined to conquer the world and force the entire populace to follow Sharia law. Islam is a political ideology masquerading as a religion and practices a cult like mentality, because any who leave Islam become known as apostates and, according to the Koran, apostates are to be killed. Because of Islam's violent ways and disdain for America, the U.S. Constitution, and the U.S. Bill of Rights, BLM has chosen to align themselves with certain Islamic groups in their efforts to overthrow that U.S. government and fundamentally transform the country. Remember when Barak Obama said he wanted to fundamentally transform the country? Maybe people should have asked what he meant, because he did not hide his Marxist leanings; even in his own autobiography he mentioned how he purposely chose the Marxist professors and students to associate with. Obama spent 20 years of his life listening to the sermons of a Black Liberation Theologist named Jeremiah Wright. Obama praised the efforts of BLM even as Ferguson, Missouri suffered from the riots that BLM instigated. Because of Obama, the Muslim Brotherhood managed to gain power in Egypt and now helps BLM, an organization that has stated that they want to fundamentally changed America.

The Muslim Brotherhood has ties to the Council for American-Islamic Relations (CAIR) which is known to have funneled money to Hamas. Hamas is a military arm of the Muslim Brotherhood. On December 2015, the Executive Director of CAIR, Nihad Awad, gave a speech to two Muslim organizations, such as, the Muslim American Society (MAS) and the Islamic Circle of North America (ICNA) where he urged American Muslims to support BLM and their cause, saying, "Black Lives Matter is our matter. Black Lives Matter is our campaign."[51] Yes, that is correct. Muslim groups that have known ties to Islamic terrorist groups overseas are encouraging American Muslims to support BLM. During this same event, Khalilah Sabra, the leader of MAS decided to go even further by comparing the current race riots that are happening in the U.S. to the Arab Spring revolutions in Egypt, Libya, Tunisia, and Syria that were led by none other, than the Muslim Brotherhood. Sabra is quoted, saying,

"We are the community that staged a revolution across the world; if we can do that, why can't we have that revolution in America?"[52]

Ask yourself, why would an Islamic terrorist group want to support BLM? Is there something more going on here?

In 2016, just before the national election Nihad Awad took his support for BLM a step further. He claimed that Muslims were the "new black people of America" and gave his allegiance to BLM. Not to be outdone, Khalilah Sabra, an American Muslim and activist, had to add her own support for BLM. She is quoted, "We are the revolutionary community that staged a revolution [caliphate] across the world. If we could do that, why can't we have that revolution in America?"[53] Yes, you read that correctly. She is calling for an Islamic revolution in the United States. We are seeing this revolution playing out now in New York city, Chicago, Minneapolis, St. Louis, and Atlanta, and it's spreading.

And this is not a lone incident of Islamic groups supporting BLM. In September 2015, BLM led a demonstration in Sacramento, CA, in favor of a bill that was to prohibit "profiling" and the CAIR chapter of California backed and attended the event. They chanted "This is what a pharaoh looks like". This was a reference to the assassination of Anwar Sadat in Egypt where people yelled "Death to Pharaoh." When BLM led protests turned riots in Ferguson, Missouri, CAIR members joined in and supported them.[54]

When BLM led a protest against a rally led by Donald Trump, they were joined by the Muslim Students Association (MSA), which is nothing more than a front for the Muslim Brotherhood.

The Islamic Republic of Iran also stands with BLM, and

Antifa for that matter. In 2016 Arab social media applauded the massacre of policemen in Dallas, Texas. A Saudi journalist, Khaled Alayan, wrote, concerning the Dallas shooting of police, that Islam "occupies the moral high ground".[55]

The Lebanese commentator, Jerry Maher, commented that, "The Dallas shooting proves that America is socially volatile and on the brink of a civil war between its different groups."[56]

Even the Ayatollah Khamenei decided to end a tweet with the Black Lives Matter hashtag after trashing the United States, by repeating the same propaganda that BLM had been spouting.[57]

As a side note, an organization to keep an eye on is the Organization for Islamic Cooperation (OIC). This is an international organization and is the second largest in the world, beaten only by the United Nations. They are hyper radical and have a shared goal with BLM: eradicating the U.S. Bill of Rights, thus eliminating many of the freedoms we enjoy in America, but want to take it a step further which would be to make Americans subordinate to Sharia Law.[58] They have been actively working to make any criticism of Islam in America to be a criminal offense. It is a safe bet that this organization has ties to the Muslim Brotherhood, and the Muslim Brotherhood, through subsidiaries, is helping BLM's movement to destroy America's capitalist society. Even though the founders of BLM are not Muslim themselves, they are accepting help from Islamic groups that support Islamic terrorism overseas in order to achieve their goals, which also follows the "by any means necessary" dictate of the Black Liberation Movement.

There is some irony here, in Islamic organizations and individual Islamists wanting to help blacks be rid of perceived oppression,—I say perceived because blacks in this country are the freest in the world, including African countries—considering that millions of Africans were enslaved for centuries by Muslims in the Arab-Muslim Slave Trade (also known as the trans-Saharan trade and Eastern slave trade), which lasted for 1300 years[59] and even funneled slaves to the Ottoman Empire. The great majority of the slaves were women and young girls who were used as sex slaves and the great majority died as a result of the Arab-Muslim Slave Trade. And it is worth noting that Muslims, especially in the Middle East, still participate in slavery even today. The Islamic world never eradicated slavery the way the United States did. It is interesting how BLM, which wants whites in America to pay reparations for American slavery, conveniently forgetting the fact that there were black slave owners and blacks who participated in the trans-Atlantic slave trade by buying and selling slaves themselves, don't see a problem with aligning themselves with Muslims, whose ancestors enslaved Africans for over a millennia and who still practice modern day slavery. You have to love the hypocrisy.

# Comply or Die: Their Tactics

*"To execute a man we don't need proof of his guilt. We
only need proof that it's necessary to execute him. It's
that simple."—Che Guevara*

Like every group bent on revolution and rooted in
Marxism, BLM practices similar tactics to ensure that
their version of history is accepted and that all dissenters and critics are silenced. They basically follow Saul Alinsky's *Rules for Radicals* and the Nazi's and Lenin's and Mao's
playbook for taking control of a country.

## Create an Enemy

First, they create a problem within your mind. What I
mean by that is they paint a picture of something that isn't
true, using one particular group as a scapegoat, and repeat
it over and over again, until you believe that the issue is real
and you support them. In the case of BLM, they chose to
focus on police brutality. The truth is, police brutality is not
some rampant problem across the U.S. nor blacks are being

hunted down and killed by the police. The facts don't support that claim, but BLM doesn't care. They have a political agenda. That doesn't mean that there are not individual instances of cops that abuse their authority, but BLM wants you to believe that if you are black or brown, the moment you step out your door some cop is just going to hunt you down and kill you, and if a cop doesn't a white person will, because according to BLM and every leftist in the country, whites are inherently racist. BLM has spent six years painting a picture of rampant police brutality that doesn't exist and of rampant racism on the part of whites that doesn't exist, but they need you to believe it does.

Hitler and the Nazis did something similar before they took power in Germany back in the 1930s. After World War I, Hitler was a nobody that had difficulty holding a job, but he found a place with the Nazi party and later became its leader. Now, history has falsely claimed that the Nazis are far right, but the truth is, they are far left. Fascists have always been far left. The Nazi party platform has a lot in common with leftist groups, such as, the socialist platform, the communist platform, the Marxist platform, BLM's platform, and the Democrat party platform. In fact, Hitler took a lot of his political ideals from the *Communist Manifesto* and if you read his *Mein Kempf*, and can get past his rantings and ravings, you'll notice the similarities. He just chose to add a more militaristic flair to his ideals.

Now, Hitler was no fool. He knew that the only way to attain power was to create division, a tactic from the *Communist Manifesto*, and he needed a boogeyman to use as a villain, so he chose the Jews. It is believed that Hitler's hatred of the Jews started when he was a child, though no one knows the exact moment that sparked his disdain for them, but when he started hating them doesn't matter; what matters is he used them as a way to gain power. For over a decade, Hitler and the Nazis painted the Jews as these evil, selfish, heartless, and inferior human beings who bled Germany dry and were the reason Germany suffered through such a terrible depression, and because of this, they deserved to pay for the wrongs they dealt to German citizens. Oftentimes, the Jews were referred to as a disease, even though the real disease is an ideology that promotes an end to individual liberty and its protections, and has to destroy an entire group of people who had done no wrong just to gain power.

Consider the following quotes.

> "For us, this is not a problem you can turn a blind eye to-one to be solved by small concessions. For us, it is a problem of whether our nation can ever recover its health, whether the Jewish spirit can ever really be eradicated. Don't be misled into thinking you can fight a disease without killing the carrier, without destroying the bacillus. Don't think you can fight racial tuberculosis without taking care to rid the nation of the carrier of that racial tuberculosis. This Jewish contamination will not subside, this poisoning of the nation will not end, until the carrier himself, the Jew, has been banished from our midst." From Hitler's speech delivered in Salzburg, 7 or 8 August 1920.[60]

> "So, we are now going to have a total solu-

*tion to the Jewish question. The programme
is clear. It reads: total separation, total segregation! What does this mean? It does not
only mean the total exclusion of the Jews
from the German economic system...    It
means much more! No German can be expected to live under the same roof as Jews.
The Jews must be chased out of our houses
and our residential districts and made to
live in rows or blocks of houses where they
can keep to themselves and come into con-
tact with Germans as little as possible. They
must be clearly identified.... And when we
compel the rich Jews to provide for the `poor'
of their race, which will certainly be necessary, they will all sink together into a pit
of criminality. As this happens, we will be
faced with the harsh necessity of eradicating
the Jewish underworld, just as we root out
criminals from our own orderly state: with
fire and sword. The result will be the certain
and absolute end of   Jewry in Germany;
its complete annihilation!" [Source: Benno
Müller-Hill. Murderous Science. New York:
CSHL Press, 1998, p.48][61]*

From Hitler's Speach in Wilhelmshaven on April1, 1939

*"Only when this Jewish bacillus infecting
the life of peoples has been removed can one
hope to establish a co-operation amongst the*

*nations which shall be built up on a lasting understanding." quoted in N H Baynes, The Speeches of Adolf Hitler, Oxford University Press, 1942, Volume I, pp.743)*[62]

Now, there was no proof that the Jews had done any of the things Hitler accused them of, but that didn't matter. People believed him and he gained a huge following. It is easy to stir up jealousy and envy and to make people hate one another, and Hitler knew this. Once he managed to gain enough of a following, he worked on making his party a prominent political force where the Nazis were able to gain seats in the German Parliament and Hitler later was made Chancellor of Germany.

BLM is just following the typical leftist playbook. First, they created an enemy: the police and white people, and all conservatives and anyone who refuses to agree with them. They claim the police are inherently racist; coined the term systemic racism, which basically means that whites are racist no matter what and that nothing is ever your fault if you're black or brown; and have spent six years calling the police scum and the private army of the Ku Klux Klan (KKK) and making you believe that, if you are black, you shouldn't call the cops because they will just kill you.

They have spent six years calling America a white, racist country that practices systemic racism and telling people of color that if they don't get that job, it because they were discriminating against you based on skin color. If a white actor is cast in a role for a movie, they immediately call it whitewashing. If anyone says that all lives should matter, they are called racist. If a white person disagrees with them, they are deemed racist, but BLM's attack on whites goes further. They call whites genetic defects and subhuman, similar to the way Hitler referred to the Jews as not being genetically pure as he promoted his Aryan race. Consider these remarks on Twitter by the co-founder of the Toronto chapter of BLM, Yusra Khogali.

> *"Whiteness is not humxness, in fact, white skin is sub-humxn. All phenotypes exist within the black family and white ppl are a genetic defect of blackness."*[63]

Or

> *"Plz Allah give me strength to not cuss/kill these men and white folks out here today."*[64]

Notice how she prays to Allah, the Muslim deity. Coincidence? Probably not. She continues her racist rants against whites calling them inferior because

> Whites *"have a higher concentration of enzyme inhibitors that suppress melanin production. They are genetically deficient because melanin is present at the inception of life."*[65]

This is not an isolated incident. Chanelle Helm, an organizer for the Louisville chapter of BLM wrote an article where she demanded reparations from all whites insinuating that whites do not deserve what they have. Her demands are as follows[66]:

1. White people, if you don't have any descendants, will your property to a black or brown family. Preferably one that lives in generational poverty.
2. White people, if you're inheriting property you intend to sell upon acceptance, give it to a black or brown family. You're bound to make that money in some other white privileged way.
3. If you are a developer or realty owner of multi-family housing, build a sustainable complex in a black or brown blighted neighborhood and let black and brown people live in it for free.
4. White people, if you can afford to downsize, give up the home you own to a black or brown family. Preferably a family from generational poverty.
5. White people, if any of the people you intend to leave your property to are racists assholes, change the will, and will your property to a black or brown family. Preferably a family from generational poverty.
6. White people, re-budget your monthly so you can donate to black funds for land purchasing.
7. White people, especially white women (because this is yaw specialty — Nosey Jenny and Meddling Kathy), get a racist fired. Yaw know what the fuck they be saying. You are complicit when you ignore them. Get your boss fired cause they racist too.
8. Backing up No. 7, this should be easy but all those sheetless Klan, Nazi's and Other lil' dick-white men will all be returning to work. Get they ass fired. Call the police even: they look suspicious.

9. OK, backing up No. 8, if any white person at your work, or as you enter in spaces and you overhear a white person praising the actions from yesterday, first, get a pic. Get their name and more info. Hell, find out where they work — Get Them Fired. But certainly address them, and, if you need to, you got hands: use them.

10. Commit to two things: Fighting white supremacy where and how you can (this doesn't mean taking up knitting, unless you're making scarves for black and brown kids in need), and funding black and brown people and their work.

In short, if you're white, you better be prepared to give up your property to your new black slave master. BLM and its followers will take it from you without impunity.

But it isn't violence against whites that is advocated. They want to abolish local police departments nationwide. This is a common tactic among communists. They always tear down the local police force of any country they invade and intend to take over, and replace it with their own officers that will make certain the populace adheres to their ideals. BLM is no different in this regard. They routinely operate through violent means and one way to ensure that they are not impeded in their goal of tearing down the United States, is to get rid of local law enforcement. This will leave people vulnerable, and they know this. Their first efforts to achieve this goal is to paint all cops as racists, including the ones that are black, of Hispanic descent, or of Asian descent. They have declared war on the police, and their efforts are gaining followers in the Democrat party and from Democrat mayors and governors across the country.

The mayor of L.A. has vowed to defund the police. New York City's mayor, de Blasio, has slashed the funding for the NYPD and slapped on so many regulations that the cops can't even do their job. The end result: police are leaving the force in droves and crime is up exponentially, but don't worry; BLM police's their own, meaning that you either follow their mandates or suffer the consequences. The Bolsheviks in Russia did this when they took over; the Nazis did this in Germany; and even Mao's Red Guard did something similar, getting rid of anyone that might stand up to them.

From the moment they first made an appearance, BLM has called for violence against the police. In 2016 in Dallas, a shooting took place where five officers were killed and others wounded. The shooter, Micah Johnson, admitted that he did it on behalf of Black Lives Matter and that he "wanted to kill white people, especially police officers". He was a black nationalist and followed the African American Defense League, which advocated for violence on police. [67]

BLM immediately claimed that they were not responsible for Johnson's actions, and though they are not directly responsible for the actions of one man, their violent rhetoric has inspired people to lash out at police and outright attack them. In BLM demonstrations across the country, the participants chant things, like, "Pigs in a blanket! Fry 'em like bacon!" or "What do we want? Dead Cops! When do we want them? Now!"[68]. Even their mantra, which is on the BLM website says, "No Justice, No Peace", which implies a move towards violence if they don't get what they want. BLM activists routinely compare the police to the KKK, and BLM activists in the United Kingdom, yes the movement has gone global, want to replace the police with a black militia, and similar calls have been made in the U.S as they believe that the only solution to ending violence in the black community is by instigating a revolution. [69] These attacks bring me to the next tactic that is used by Marxists.

## Violence

Violence is a common companion of Marxists because it is the only way they manage to gain power. The Nazis used violence to shut down their critics. News organizations that printed anything critical of Hitler suddenly found themselves literally burnt to the ground, and the fear such tactics generated cornered them into silence. The communists that took over Russia and murdered Czar Nikolas and his family used violence to get what they wanted. They, too, burned down stores, attacked people in the streets and created an atmosphere of fear. The Red Guard under Mao Zedong during the communist takeover of China ripped people from their homes and executed them in the streets as a warning to anyone who even thought about fighting back. BLM is no different.

In the last six weeks or more BLM activists have burned down department stores, looted these same stores, attacked cops, thrown Molotov cocktails, pulled truckers out of their trucks and beat them within an inch of their life, if not killing them outright, and murdered others in the streets. Can you be surprised that they act with violence when their leaders say things like the following?

> *"Whatever you do, you pull your pistol out and f\*cking bust them... Trust me when you see me move, I'm moving in violence.*

*We need action. I don't give a f\*ck if you
knock them over, whether you run up on
them, whatever you do, you better f\*cking
take action.*"[70]

BLM activists took over a Target store in Washington
D.C., vowing to shut them down if they called the police with
the leader, saying "All black people, living around this neighborhood, living around in this neighborhood, because you
prioritize money over people, so until you stop calling the
police, we continue to shut your business down."[71]

After Rayshard Brooks was shot and killed by a police
officer in Atlanta, Georgia, fueled by the actions of BLM activists across the country, people immediately burned down
the Wendy's where the incident took place, and proceeded
to block an interstate, calling for justice. It didn't matter that
Brooks attacked two officers, stole one officer's taser, and
then tried to shoot the office with the taser, which resulted in
him being shot and killed.[72] BLM activists burned the Wendy's to the ground, putting employees out of work, some of
whom were black.

The followers of the "No Justice, No Peace," mantra are
making good on their promise. That location has become a
focal point for BLM protests, and on July Fourth weekend
2020, two people opened fire on passing cars which resulted
in an eight-year-old girl being killed. The mother of the child
issued a statement, "They say Black Lives Matter. You killed
your own. They killed my baby because she crossed a barrier
and made a U-turn? You killed a child. She didn't do nothing
to nobody. Black Lives Matter? You killing your own. You
killed an 8-year-old child. She ain't did nothing to no one of

y'all. She just wanted to get home to see her cousin. That's all she wanted to do."[73]

In Provo, Utah, a BLM member opened fire on a vehicle that drove through a BLM protest in an attempt to get to the connecting street, wounding the driver. The shooter just went back to protesting after he emptied his weapon.[74] Where is the denunciation from BLM?

BLM says they want peace, yet they never condemn the violence that is done by their followers.

## Eradicate the Past

Communists always remove reminders of the past as a way of controlling the collective thoughts and wants of the people they wish to control. Karl Marx said it best, "If you can cut the people off from their history, then they can be easily persuaded." To which he added, "Take away a nation's heritage and they are more easily persuaded."[75] Why do you think BLM in coalition with Antifa is trying to tear down monuments to America's past and heritage? It's a strategic move. When the Bolsheviks took over Russia, they tore down every statue, every essence of Russian history that might remind the Russian people that there was a time before the Soviets reigned supreme. This is done on purpose. They need people to forget the past, so that they have nothing to compare their current circumstances to, but it also makes it easier to control the minds of the youth because there will be no evidence that anything existed before the state.

When the Nazis took over Germany, they removed statues of Germany's past and erected statues glorifying the Third Reich and its Fuhrer. They took away the art so that no German citizen could see it, replacing it with the approved art of the Reich. Here is where the Nazis differed from the

Bolsheviks and the Red Guard, instead of destroying the art they tore down, many of the high ranking Nazi officers and members of the SS kept the art for themselves, but they made certain that all the average citizen saw was the Swastika, just like in the Soviet Union the hammer and sickle was everywhere.

Mao used his Red Guard to conduct the cultural revolution where Chinese art from the past and all reminders that China had been a more democratic, capitalist society was eradicated. Any caught trying to preserve pre-communist Chinese culture was executed. The revolution itself began in 1966 and ended in 1976 with the death of Mao himself. By that time, an estimated five to ten million people had been massacred in the name of preserving communist thought and enacting the Maoist Doctrine.[76]

University professors, the middle class, business owners, and anyone who wasn't communist enough were sent to the countryside to be farmers and reeducated so as to purge them of their bourgeoisie ways and thoughts. The lucky ones were executed right away instead of being forced to suffer in complete poverty and despair with the constant threat of torture for themselves or their families if they failed to comply with the Red Guard's demands. And though China has moved away from some of Mao's ideas, they still hold to the communist idea that everything is controlled by the state, and freedom of thought, as with any form of dissent, is not allowed. They control what their people can read on the internet, which Google® is helping them with, and have what is called a social credit system, where if you do anything the state deems distasteful, you get a low score, and a low score means that your opportunities in life (education, career, housing) are severely limited if not outright denied.

BLM is merely following the communist playbook in tearing down statues across the United States in the name of ending racism. Every statue has been deemed racist, but what they are really doing is tearing down reminders of our past. It started with Confederate statues because most people were in agreement that maybe having statues that glorified the heroes of the South, where slavery was legal until the end of the Civil War (1860-1865), might not be a good idea. But the statue eradication has moved to tearing down statues of Christopher Columbus (founder of the New World—yes he is the founder of the New World—which led to the eventual colonization of the east coast by England; which led to the eventual formation of the United States, a country founded upon and always striving to achieve the principles of individual liberty and God given rights); George Washington (leader of the Continental Army, president of the Constitutional Convention, first president of the United States, and literally the main reason America even exists, allowing us to outlaw slavery and become a world power that helped defeat the fascists of Germany, Italy and Japan during WWII); Ulysses S. Grant (leader of the Union Army that defeated the South and helped end slavery); a memorial to the 54th Massachusetts Regiment (the first all-black regiment of the Union Army that fought against the South); Abraham Lincoln (president of the United States during the Civil War and who ushered the Emancipation Proclamation, and this particular statue was erected by former slaves and Frederick Douglas, a former slave, gave the commemoration to it); and Theodore Roosevelt (who fought for worker's rights in the early 20th century and instituted the National Park system to preserve the natural beauty of America's land) to name a few.

However, BLM sees no problem with a statue commemorating the works of Karl Marx or of Vladimir Lenin remaining up, even though their ideology and actions have resulted in the death of nations, the death of millions worldwide, and the forcing of people into poverty, nor are they concerned about the fact that Marx thought those of the black race were inferior.

The tearing down of statues is not about fighting racism. That is nice euphemism for wanting to tear down vestiges of America's past, because as far as BLM and its followers are concerned, all of America is racist and America never had a right to exist. One thing they are forgetting is that, without America, none of them would be here. They either wouldn't exist, or would be living in countries that do not tolerate freedom of speech the way America does. The true goal of BLM is the complete eradication of the United States itself, with them setting up their own government in its stead, one that is predicated upon race. They want to implement the very wrongs they accuse all Americans, especially American whites, of having committed.

But they aren't stopping at statues. Activists have decided that Aunt Jemima pancakes should no longer exist, and as a result, the logo and name is being changed by Quaker Oats, the current owner of Aunt Jemima pancake mix. They called her face on a box of pancake mix and syrup racist, not giving a damn about the history of the original face behind it, simply because, according to them, it glorifies the "mammy" character, therefore it is racist.

The original Aunt Jemima, or rather the first individual to portray the character, was a former slave named Nancy Green who was hired to help market a ready-made pancake mix by the R. T. Davis Milling Company. She portrayed the character in real life and on film reels of the day. The woman went from former slave to an employee at a major company where she worked as a storyteller, actress, and a singer. She was originally hired to sell pancakes at the World's Columbian Exposition in Chicago in 1893, and it turned out that she was very good at it to the point that her booth drew the most visitors. She was signed to a lifelong contract and later died in 1923 in a car accident. She became one of the first corporate models for blacks in America by becoming the first black woman to be hired as a corporate representative. This was quite an achievement, considering the time period, and allowed her to fight the racial stereotypes of her day. She also used her Aunt Jemima caricature to raise millions of dollars for various charities that helped the underprivileged.[77] It is a great America success story that demonstrated how even a black woman can find success, and she did more good portraying a character, than any BLM activist does by tearing down statues or get logos changed. But BLM has decided that her story is racist and should not be told.

Of course, activists have also decided that the logos of Uncle Ben's rice and Cream of Wheat are racist and also need to go. But removing icons on food items doesn't promote black lives. All it does is remove what has become an integral part of American culture, great food that you can prepare quickly and easily without spending too much time or effort. Most Americans never thought of the icons on these foods as racist, until recently; instead, they were viewed as symbols for good food.

These same activists have decided that *Gone With the Wind* is racist because of Haddie McDaniel's portrayal of the "mammy" character. But how is it racist? According to them it promotes a stereotype, but it is clear that the people wanting the movie removed from streaming channels have never watched it. *Gone With the Wind* (released in 1939) gives a bit of a glorified portrayal of the Old South, but that's about it. It also shows the realities of war and what the Civil War did to, not just the South, but the country as a whole. The "mammy" character in the movie is a sassy, no nonsense woman, who does not like being talked back to and will dish it right back out when anyone gives her an attitude. She is basically a strong-willed individual who learns to survive in the circumstances she finds herself in, and she constantly gives a tongue lashing to the white protagonist, Scarlett O'Hara, who is portrayed as a spoiled rotten, self-centered, brat who cares only for herself and her own desires. Haddie McDaniel won an Oscar for her portrayal of the "mammy" character, and was the first black person, and first black female, to receive such an honor. Instead of celebrating such an achievement, modern Marxists want it erased.

But, again, BLM is not interested fighting real racism, because if they were, they would chuck the racists out of their own organization. They are only interested in getting America's culture to change. They want businesses to bend to their will, which is a typical communist tactic. And so far, they are succeeding.

## Give me your child, and I will have the perfect communist.

Children are often used by Marxists to achieve their ends because they are so malleable. Karl Marx said, "The education of all children, from the moment that they can get along without a mother's care, shall be in state institutions." The reason for this is that the only way Marxists can keep their ideology alive is by indoctrinating children in it.[78]

Stalin once said that, "Education is a weapon whose effects depend on who holds it in his hands and at whom it is aimed."[79] Such a statement is very true. Whoever controls the education of the youth, controls the future, and this has always been a tenet of Marxism and one that BLM is making good use of. When Vladimir Lenin took over Russia, renamed The Soviet Union, after the Bolshevik Revolution of 1917, he implemented youth programs to indoctrinate children in the ideals of communism, knowing that they needed to be radicalized, and their youthful fervor guided to promote the communist state. Stalin perfected this model, understanding full-well how important it was to make sure that children were well-programmed to accept and defend communism. This happened through organizations aimed at the youth: Komsomol, Young Pioneers, and Little Octobrists.[80] These organizations focused on educating children in communist propaganda and instilling in them a severe hatred for capitalism, and especially, for America.

Hitler did the same thing with his Hitler Youth. All children were required to join. They would play games, participate in physical exercise, the boys learned to fight, the girls learned domestic duties, but all of them were indoctrinated with Nazi propaganda about the purity of the Aryan race, antisemitic sentiments, and how the Reich should be defended and never questioned.

Mao did the same with his Red Guard, choosing to focus on recruiting youth, especially college age youth, who would carry out communist dictates with enthusiasm and do as they were told, without question. Many of the youth in China during the Cultural Revolution turned on their own professors who had already indoctrinated them with communist propaganda. The students in these communist schools not only turned on their professors, but on their friends, and parents. Basically, they turned on anyone who did not believe as they did. It is reported that some of these radicalized youth literally ate their professors because the professors were not radical enough, and therefore, deemed traitors. This is what communism, in all of its forms, creates. Literal and metaphorical cannibalism.

James David Banker, an author who wrote about China's Cultural Revolution and was published by Quillette Magazine, once wrote, regarding China's communist schools,

> *"Mao's decision to use China's youth as his vanguard was, by fortune or foresight, instrumental to the revolution's initial success. The young may be pure in heart, but they are also high on emotion and short on life experience. Simply put, they are natural philistines. Still in their identity-forming years, China's young had few barriers to a complete identification with the Red Guards. Conformity and intolerance of dissent followed naturally. [snip] With undeveloped mental immune systems, their soft skulls were fertile ground for Mao's secular Manichaeism. Manichaeism reduces society, with all the diversity and complexity of human experience, to a blunt dichotomy:*

*light and darkness, good and evil, right and wrong, radical and reactionary. "There is no middle way!" became a popular slogan. Ideologies like these are intellectually and morally vapid, yet their simplicity and certainty are alluring, especially to the young. Thus, Mao's child revolutionaries could—with youthful exuberance and clarity of purpose—chain a teacher to a radiator and bludgeon him to death with an iron bar, or force a teacher to eat nails and feces, among other tortures."[81]*

And it continues.

*"In the years prior to the Cultural Revolution, the Party had cultivated an environment of extreme political conformity. Political rallies and self-criticism sessions had become a regular feature of Maoist thought-reform campaigns."[82]*

Sound familiar? Are we not experiencing an age of extreme political conformity? Anyone who goes against the left is smeared on Twitter, risks losing their job, and faces a severe backlash. Think of the BLM protests where white professors and youth decided to shackle themselves in the same manner slaves were chained as a profession of their guilt for being white, kind of like a "self-criticism session". Well, there is more.

*"Eating human flesh became a macabre*

*proof of loyalty. The Party's own investiga-*
*tions tell of students in Guangxi province*
*cooking and eating their teachers and prin-*
*cipals. In some government cafeterias, the*
*bodies of executed traitors were displayed*
*on meat hooks, while their flesh was served*
*and consumed. The blank slate, it seems,*
*can also be a dark abyss."[83]*

We are seeing this cultural revolution in the United States thanks to groups like BLM. BLM wants whites to apologize for being white, because, just by being born white, they are racist and responsible for slavery, even though slavery in the U.S. ended in 1865. They want whites to castrate themselves on the altar of racial justice and pay for sins they never committed, and they want all of America to apologize for America's existence and exploitation of other countries, even though the U.S. gives billions away in foreign aid and allows the most immigrants into the country and also allows them to collect some form of welfare.

Just like the Nazis and the Communists of China and Russia (North Korea, Venezuela, and Cuba can also be included), BLM is after your kids to train them in Marxist ideology based on racial segregation. Think it hasn't happened? Think again.

New York City has decided to roll out a Black Lives Matter themed lesson plan that will be taught in all of their schools, staring the fall semester of 2020. According to the New York public education board the lesson plan will explore police brutality, systemic racism, and white privilege. If you are white, be prepared to have your kids come home in tears for being told how evil they are.[84]

The 1619 Project, published by the New York Times, is going to be taught in schools across the nation, even though history professors have said that it is full of inaccuracies.

Wake County in North Caroline has already launched a website with online resources and BLM prepared lesson plans for teachers to use in their classrooms to "address the injustices that exist beyond education by the conversations we have with others, by speaking up when we see hate, by supporting efforts that oppose racism and oppression, and by directly engaging in advocacy work."[85] This lesson plan has three steps: "Step one: Recognize your white privilege. Step two: Learn the dos and don'ts of being an ally. Step three: Recruit more members to learn steps one and two."[86] This is textbook Marxism!

KIPP Philadelphia Public Schools has decided to implement their own lesson plan that they admit is rooted in Black Liberation Theology. As explained before, the Black Liberation Movement is a Marxist movement that promotes black supremacy and plans to institute their vision for America by any means necessary. According to their site, they wish to achieve "education equity" and believe Black Lives Matter. They have come up with a plan to root out any racism in their schools. These are the changes they plan to implement (emphasis added)[87]:

- "ALL of our team members must constantly engage in the process of **unlearning mindsets and practices rooted in anti-Blackness** and **learning mindsets and practices rooted in Black liberation.** We prioritize robust staff development and training in a shared school vision, curriculum, theory, culturally responsive practices, and instructional leadership."

- "Our students, most of whom are Black, are at the center of our work. Applying intense and sustained pressure to the systems that marginalize them and their families is core to ensuring their safety, well-being, and positive educational outcomes. This *pressure must be applied both locally and nationally.*"

- "We are investing resources in *building out our practices in social emotional learning and trauma-informed teaching and supports.* Because of the systemic inequities in our country and our city, we know that our students face additional challenges to achieving their dreams so we are doing everything we can to remove all barriers and lift our students up, both academically and emotionally."

- "We *engage and work with community leaders* to provide countless resources to our students and families. *We invite lawmakers, activists, and changemakers into our classrooms and community* to show our students that their voice matters."

- "We show up for our families. Currently, we are hosting town halls and utilize surveys to understand the needs of our community. They are the leading voice at our decision-making table. This ensures that we can provide the support that's needed and if we can't provide it, *we will connect our families to community organizations and city resources* that can."

They are admitting that they will be teaching children

BLM propaganda and they intend to make it a national requirement for all schools to do the same. Textbook Marxism. But this has been going on for a while.

In Durham, North Carolina, at Central Park School, a First-Grade teach took her students to a Black Lives Matter rally in 2016. The teacher's name is Stef Bernal-Martinez and she is a self-described "Radical Queer Progressive Educator" and "white-passing Xicana."[88] This woman should not be a teacher as it is clear that she cannot and refuses to keep her politics out of the classroom. Instead of teaching her students how to read and spell, she decided to train them in how to be perfect little Marxists and champions of the cause. She has bragged about training new activists and no consent forms were sent to the parents. The students wore Black Lives Matter t-shirts to the march and those shirts were donated by an anonymous donor. How interesting.

This move to inculcate children in BLM propaganda is nationwide. In San Francisco, the school board has decided to start an ethnic studies program in order to instruct students about structural racism, identity, and social justice. The plan is called the Equity Studies to Implement Humanizing Learning Experiences for All Students and it would commit the San Francisco Unified School District to focus its curriculum on being "'decolonizing and anti-oppressive' pedagogy and a 'humanizing' framework for teaching students based on three guiding principles: self-love and knowledge, solidarity between communities and self-determination."[89]

The words decolonizing and anti-oppressive are codewords for being anti-American, anti-Western Civilization, anti-white, and will focus on the idea that America is inherently racist, that blacks are oppressed, and that because the system is unfair to people of color, it needs to be torn down and replaced. Self-love refers to building self-esteem instead of instilling discipline and the idea that you must work for something in order to achieve it. And "solidarity between communities" is a nice way of saying that students will be learning how to organize and work together as activists in order to bring about the Marxist revolution in America. In addition to this proposal, a group of librarians in the school district compiled a series of lessons that teaches kids about the BLM movement, consisting of videos, graphics, grand jury documents, poetry readings, lesson plans, readings, and activities for students of all ages.[90]

But this goes beyond the schools. There are BLM reading lists for kids, BLM coloring books, and even a Black Lives Matter for Kids[91] website that promotes the idea that there is systemic racism in America while portraying BLM activists as peaceful protestors, leaving out the fact that wherever they show up property gets damaged, people get hurt, or that their members promote the idea that whites are inferior to nonwhites. Basically, it gives a very watered-down version of BLM as a way to lure children and parents into the movement. The Black Lives Matter coloring book was created to be used as a tool by parents and teachers to teach children about the core principles of BLM and to have "conversations about race" which centers around the idea that blacks are oppressed and whites are the oppressors.[92]

Milwaukee Public Schools implemented a Black Lives Matter Week of Action event which took place February 3, 2020 to February 7, 2020. The week consisted of events, such as, Storytelling and Social Awards Night, Black Lives Matter Poetry and Open Mic, The Criminalization of Black Girls in

School, Wisconsin Black Historical Society & Museum, and Students' Education Amplified–Student-Led Discussion and Live Broadcast.[93] It was a free event, meant to lure parents and their children in so that they can learn how to "bring about positive change", which is code for learning how to be an activist.

BLM has followed what many Marxists, communists, Maoists, Nazis, and socialists—they are all threads of the same cloth—have done before: they have infiltrated the schools and convinced school districts to teach their ideology to children, allowing them a chance to turn children—your children—into perfect BLM activists. It's a perfect set-up, and it has gone under the radar.

## Dissent Not Allowed

Another tactic of BLM, like all Marxists, is to shut down any criticism and dissent. They believe in tolerance and peace, so long as you comply with their demands and accept their mandates, but if you don't, they shut you down. They live by a comply or die philosophy.

After the Bolshevik Revolution of 1917, Lenin declared himself the leader of Russia, but Russians everywhere disagreed with him. In fact, most Russians were not for the Bolshevik Revolution at all, but they didn't do anything to stop it either, viewing it more as a fringe group. They learned the hard way that one should never underestimate the lengths in which communists are willing to go to achieve power and absolute control over others' lives. This is why, beginning in 1918, Lenin instituted what became known as the Red Terror, and for four years, until 1922, blood reigned in Russia, or the newly formed Soviet Union. In short, Lenin gave an order to his followers to get rid of all dissenters by force, or by any means necessary. Any who did not adhere to the communist party line was hung in public, their name released, and their grain seized. The most minor infraction could lead to death. Lenin believed that anything was permissible in the name of revolution and allowed his followers to run amok, dispensing any punishment they want to those who weren't communist enough. Lenin is quoted as saying, "For us, all is permitted. Let there be blood."[94]

Under Hitler, the Nazis tortured and killed any who criticized them. The SS was well-known for their methods in extracting information so as to be able to round up any who might prove problematic for the Third Reich. When Hitler gained power, opposition to Nazism was outlawed and the idea of freedom of speech eradicated. Dissenters were rounded up and put into concentration camps. Sometimes they were just publicly executed. When Hitler got the Enabling Act passed in Germany, which he did through intimidation and threats, he was granted extraordinary power to basically do what he wanted without having to go through the German President, thus sealing his power over Germany. Any suspected dissenters were fired from their civil service positions, Jews were also fired, and unionization was outlawed so as to quell any chance of opposition to his rule. Violence, intimidation, oppression, and harassment became the norm as dissenters were systematically rounded up and disposed of. Once the Nazis secured their authority over Germany, they kept it by silencing any who opposed them.[95]

Mao Zedong's Red Guard was notorious for shutting down dissenters. Any who did not accept the communist party in China was tortured or killed or both. It wasn't unusual for Red Guard members to pull people from their homes and execute them in the streets. Freedom of the press and of speech were outlawed. The state was everything. Dissent was and still is outlawed in China. Recently, China passed a law and created a taskforce that is supposed to "Build a Peaceful China" as a response to the Hong Kong protestors of 2019 and critics of their response to the coronavirus pandemic. The purpose of the taskforce and the law accompanying it is to stifle any dissent and criticism of the Communist Party and President Xi Jinping. A man was arrested for carrying a Hong Kong Flag.[96]

Look at North Korea, Cuba, and Venezuela; any political dissent results in arrests and executions. Look at the Islamic countries where Sharia law reigns supreme. Any who contest Sharia is executed. Contrary thought is not allowed. All are expected to conform. The only way out is death, similar to that of a cult, and if you think about it, Marxism, in all of its forms, is a cult-like mentality.

Che Guevara was an Argentine Marxist who played an important role in the Cuban revolution of the 1960s and who disposed of his dissenters without mercy. The man was ruthless and dealt with opposition swiftly, not caring if innocents died. He is quoted,

> *"We executed many people by firing squad without knowing if they were fully guilty. At times, the Revolution cannot stop to conduct much investigation."*[97]

He called the very notion of a trial or burden of proof as an "archaic bourgeois detail". In December of 1964, Guevara gave a speech to the United Nations in which he admitted, "Yes, we have executed, we are executing, and we will continue to execute."[98] Guevara was indiscriminate when it came to killing. He loved murder and was nothing more than a cold-blooded killer who got some sort of psychedelic high from executing people. In short, he was a man with no soul and believed that the communist revolution should be won by any means necessary, and the more killing, the better. He wrote to his father once,

> *"My nostrils dilate while savoring the acrid odor of gunpowder and blood...I'd like to confess, Papa, at that moment I discovered that I really like killing."[99]*

Freedom of speech? Not in Guevara's world. Anyone could be sent to a reeducation camp, i.e. his version of a concentration camp, for the most minor of offenses, and homosexuals were either executed on the spot, or sent to a camp where they performed hard labor in the harshest of conditions. This is why I shake my head anytime I see someone form the LGBT movement wearing a Che Guevara shirt; the man despised homosexuals, believing that they were not worthy of being treated as human beings.

Now we have BLM, another Marxist revolutionary group that wants to usher in change, and one way they do it is by getting rid of dissent. Like all Marxists, they cannot stand it when anyone disagrees with them or questions them. The moment you stand against them, or even say, "all lives matter" you are targeted by BLM.

The principle of Windsor High School, in Windsor, Vermont was fired for not supporting BLM wholeheartedly. She published a Facebook post where she questioned their methods, and for that she was fired. She wrote, "I DO NOT agree with coercive measures taken to get this point across; some of which are falsified in an attempt to prove a point. I do not think that people should be made to feel they have to choose black race over human race. While I understand the urgency to feel compelled to advocate for black lives, what about our law enforcement?"[100] She even had the audacity to say that she is not a racist just because she refuses to walk around with a Black Lives Matter sign. Such thought is not allowed, according to BLM.

Here is a short list of people who have lost their jobs because they criticized BLM, or said something BLM did not like.[101]

- Editor-in-chief at *Variety*, Claudia Eller, posted a Tweet about a dispute she had with someone because the person thought her piece on the lack of diversity at the magazine she worked for wasn't good enough.
- An editor at the *Philidelphis Inquirer*, Stan Wischnowski, ran a headline that read, "Buildings Matter, Too," and was fired.
- NBA announcer Grant Napear was fired from his sports talk radio program and was forced to resign form his position as announcer for the Sacramento Kings because he tweeted, "All live matter."
- *Bon Appétit* editor-in-chief Adam Rapoport was forced to resign after he published a piece that was apologetic toward BLM, but was

deemed as unapologetic enough. It also didn't help that an old photo of him going as black-face for Halloween one year surfaced.

- At UCLA, a professor refused to cancel final exams for his students, following the death of George Floyd, and was placed on permanent leave.
- When a reporter in Wales complained that BLM activists were not following the country's social distancing rules, he was forced to step down as a judge for Wales Book of the Year.
- A member pf MTV's *The Challenge* tweeted, "people die every f–king day" after initial protests, soon turned riots, over George Floyd's death was fired.
- Aleksander Katai, a professional soccer player, was let go from his team, LA Galaxy, because his wife criticized BLM on Instagram.
- A Canadian cabinet minister expressed his belief that he doesn't believe Canada was a racist country, and for that, he was fired from three separate jobs.

But firing those they don't like BLM doesn't stop at editors, talk show hosts, or actors. A Catholic priest, Father Theodore Rothrock, at the Diocese of Lafayette, Indiana was suspended for criticizing BLM. He wrote in a bulletin, "Who are the real racists and the purveyors of hate? You shall know them by their works. The only lives that matter are their own and the only power they seek is their own. They are wolves in wolves clothing, masked thieves and bandits, seeking only to devour the life of the poor and profit from the fear of others. They are maggots and parasites at best, feeding off the isolation of addiction and broken families, and offering to replace any current frustration and anxiety with more misery and greater resentment."[102]

Further on, he wrote, "Black Lives Matter, Antifa, and the other nefarious acolytes of their persuasion are not the friends or allies we have been led to believe. They are serpents in the garden, seeking only to uproot and replant a new species of human made in the likeness of men and not in the image of God."[103]

Adding, "Their poison is more toxic than any pandemic we have endured. The father of lies has not just been seen in our streets, we have invited him into our home. Now he is prowling like a roaring lion looking for someone to devour. Resist him, strong in your faith."

He concluded, "What would the great visionary leaders of the past be contributing to the discussion at this point in time?" he asked. "Would men like Fredrick Douglas [sic] and the Reverend King, both men of deep faith, be throwing bombs or even marching in the streets? Would they be pleased with the murder rates in our cities or the destruction of our families by the welfare system? Would they see a value in the obliteration of our history to re-write a future without the experience and struggles of the past? Would we tear down their monuments?"[104]

Everything the priest said is true, but because he criticized BLM, and Antifa, he has been suspended.

Incidents like the above are happening all over America, and the world. Criticize BLM and lose your job. Criticize BLM, and you may lose your life. This is an effective way to shut down opposition. If you refuse to support BLM, you are branded a racist and fired, or killed. No exceptions. This is how BLM operates.

But BLM has moved from punishing the influential who do not bow to their demands. They now go after everyday citizens. When two people painted over a BLM mural, they were arrested for a hate crime. A student at the University of Houston was punished for posting "All lives matter" on social media. People who challenge BLM get beat up in the streets. You don't need to even challenge them. Get in their way and they take you out. There are plenty of videos on YouTube of BLM activists knocking cameras out of people's hands for daring to film them. Stand against BLM, it may be the last thing you do.

Nothing makes the last point more potent than the BLM activists that did resort to murder. A woman and her fiancé had an altercation with BLM activists. The BLM members drew weapons, prompting the woman's fiancé to draw his weapon as well, which forced the BLM members to walk away. According to the woman's fiancé, she had yelled after them that "all lives matter".[105] At some point, the BLM activists caught up with the woman and her fiancé again and opened fire, shooting her in the head multiple times, thus killing her. Her crime? Standing up to BLM.

A group like BLM does not stop at just firing oppositionists to their movement, they soon will be calling for executions. In fact, some members already have. This is textbook Marxism: shut down the opposition by any means necessary.

# Powerful Benefactors

*"The last capitalist we hang shall be the one who sold us the rope." —Karl Marx*

For a nonprofit organization, BLM seems to have a l lot of money. They have an alliance with "ThousandCurrents", which is a tax-exempt organization that claims to be a charity, but supports far-left causes. ActBlue also handles any donations made through the BLM website and donations made to other far-left organizations where it takes a cut as a fee for handling the money, after which, some of that money seems to go to "ThousandCurrents" and later BLM, but since they are nonprofit, they don't have to disclose where they send the funds or who gives them funds. Black Lives Matter Global—remember Black Matters is a global organization, which is a bit strange for something that is supposed to be grassroots—receives millions of dollars and 71% of that goes to their consultants and salaries.[106] Interesting thing is that Susan Rosenberg is a board member for "Thousand-Currents". Rosenberg serves as the Prisoner Rights Advocate and Writer Thousand Currents Vice-Chair of the Board of Directors where she is a "human rights and prisoner rights advocate, adjunct professor, communications consultant, award-winning writer, public speaker, and a formerly incarcerated person". She is a former member of the Weather Underground and served 16 years in a federal prison for her role in the 1983 bombing of the U.S. Capitol Building, New York Patrolmen's Benevolent Association, and the Naval War College, until Bill Clinton pardoned her in 2001, and she has never apologized for her actions.[107]

Besides the possibility that money is being funneled to them, another reason BLM is such a powerful political movement that has managed to spread everywhere within our society in such a short span of time is because they are well-funded by some powerful benefactors. They are not a grassroots movement. They never were. They were founded by professional activists who are part of other leftist organizations that promote black power and racial justice. Thy know how to organize, and the evidence of that can be seen in video after video of BLM activists working alongside Antifa activists to destroy businesses and cause as much chaos as they can in order to demoralize and weaken America. So, is it any surprise that they seem to have all the money in the world?

Their number one benefactor is George Soros, the multi billionaire that made his billions by collapsing the economies of other countries, and turns around and uses those billions to reshape the world into his image. For a long while, he has had his eyes set on transforming the United States into a Marxist nightmare. He despises the America ideal of individual liberty of everyone, or that people have the right to live their lives free from fear and oppression. Now, before you start rolling your eyes and screaming that America is racist and had slaves, think about this: the ideal of individual liberty for all led the U.S. to end slavery at a time when it was considered the norm, to pass laws ensuring that all citizens are allowed to vote, and to routinely fight for the rights of individuals not just here, but around the world. The U.S. is the most liberal, and I mean that in the traditional sense, country in the world whose citizens are the freest. But groups like BLM, funded by people like George Soros want to end that.

Soros has his hands in almost everything that plagues this country, and the world, and he does this through various foundations, totaling about 206, that he funds. Soros funneled money to the BLM movement through his Open Society Foundation to the tune of $33 million in grants,[108] but he didn't stop there, because he has since given $220 million[109] to radical groups that are just like BLM, all in the name of promoting racial justice. Remember, racial justice is not about achieving equality between people of different racial backgrounds; it's about pitting people against each other to create conflict as a way of overthrowing the system. These funds are all sent by the Open Society Foundation, which is Soros' own foundation, and some of the groups being funded are: Black Voters Matter, Repairers of The Breach, Circle For Innovations, and the Equal Justice Initiative—all of which are part of the BLM movement.[110] The main stream media (MSM) loves to report that Soros funding BLM is all rumor, but they also promote the idea that he is a philanthropist while ignoring how he actually made his money and that all of the organizations he funds promote left-wing causes and are political movements. DCLeaks.com actually posted documents that showed that the Open Society Foundation gave about $650,000 to BLM directly.[111]

The Center for American Progress also gives grants to the BLM movement and receives funding from George Soros. This is how Soros is funding BLM.[112]

The Ford Foundation created the Black-Led Movement Fund (BLMF) and has raised $100 million[113] for the Movement for Black Lives coalition, all of which is part of the BLM movement. BLM may not be getting the money directly, but they have helped create other groups that are part of their movement and promote the same goals. Keep in mind that Black Lives Matter is more than just a single group, it is an entire political movement that spans the globe. The purpose of the BLMF is to partner with the BLM movement and they do this, in part, by funding the Movement for Black Lives[114], which is a subsidiary of BLM itself, and has demanded "collective liberation" for the black community. It's the more radical arm of an already radical organization. And notice the use of the word collective. Only Marxists talk in terms of collective rights, collective action, collective liberation, because everything is about the group, not the individual.

> "We'll provide long-term support to the Movement for Black Lives, so that these visionary leaders and organizations can continue to cultivate and maintain a movement of young black women and men who are pushing through established boundaries as they seek to realize the promise of equality and justice for all. That is what democracy needs to function—and it's what the

*Movement for Black Lives is doing." –From the Ford Foundation Website.*[115]

Other companies funding and promoting the BLM movement are

- Nike, which announced that it would give $40 million over the course of four years to the black community in the name of fighting racial injustice, which is part of the BLM movement.[116]
- Apple has pledged $100 million to the Racial Equity and Justice Initiative. According to their CEO Tim Cook, it will "challenge the systemic barriers to opportunity and dignity that exist for communities of color, and particularly for the black community."[117]
- Google has given $12 million to the BLM cause.[118]
- Microsoft[119]
- Netflix has basically vowed to allow their platform to be used for the Black Lives Matter cause.[120]
- Spotify[121]
- Amazon[122]
- Snap[123]
- Airbnb[124]
- Away (luggage brand)[125]
- Facebook. Zuckerberg promised to give $10 million to the cause of fighting racial justice. It is safe to say that BLM will benefit from that in some way.[126]

- Glossier (beauty brand)[127]
- Warby Parker (eyeglass seller) is donating funds to various organizations in the name of fighting systemic racism.[128]
- Walmart has pledged $100 million over the next five years to the BLM movement.[129]
- Home Depot's CEO has pledged $1 million to Civil Rights Under Law and has vowed to ensure that the company works internally to fight systemic racism and have internal town halls where people can come together and achieve a better understanding on racial bias under the guise of understanding one another. [130]
- Target is giving $10 million to advance social justice, which is part of the BLM movement, through their supporting partners of the National Urban League and the African American Leadership Forum. They have also pledged to give pro-bono consulting to black owned businesses to the tune of 10,000 hours. Now, there is nothing wrong with Target wanting to help black owned businesses, but they aren't doing this because they believe in helping them; they just want to get onto the BLM bandwagon which fuels the BLM movement.[131]
- Gaming companies, such as, Square Enix ($250,000 direct donation to BLM), Ubisoft ($100,000 to NAACP and BLM), and EA Games ($1 million) are giving money to the cause. [132]

- Clothing and accessories retailers, such as, Etsy ($500,000 each to both the Equal Justice Initiative and the Borealis Philanthropy's Black-Led Movement Fund), H&M (4500,000 divided among NAACP, ACLU and Color of Change), Toms Shoes ($100,000 to organizations that support the BLM cause), Everlance ($75,000 to Equal Justice Initiative and the ACLU and teaching materials for how to get involved with the BLM movement), Spanx ($100,000 to Black Lives Matter, NAACP Legal Defense and Education Fund and The Minnesota Freedom Fund and $100,000 to local organizations that support the BLM cause), Levis ($200,000 to the BLM movement), and GAP brands ($250,000 to Embrace Race and the NAACP), Lululemon ($100,000 to the Minnesota Freedom Fund and $250,000 to other organizations including Black Lives Matter, NAACP, and Reclaim the Block).[133]

- Restaurants and food brands, such as, Wendy's ($500,000 to support social justice and education in the black community, but I have my doubts that that money will be used to teach children how to read and do basic math), McDonald's ($1 million to the National Urban League and NAACP), and Coca Cola ($2.5 million for social justice, including the Equal Justice Initiative, NAACP, National Center for Civil and Human Rights).[134]

- Companies that sell beauty products, such as, Honest Beauty ($100,000 to the NAACP Legal Defense Fund and the Equal Justice Initiative), Anastasia Beauty ($100,000 each to The Innocence Project, Black Live Matter, the NAACP Legal Defense and Education Fund, The Marshall Project, and Black Visions Collective), and Glossier ($500,000 to organizations "focused on combating racial injustice," and another $500,000 to black-owned beauty products).[135]
- Health and wellness companies, such as, Whoop ($20,000 to the Equal Justice Initiative), UnitedHealth Group ($10 million for George Floyd's children and businesses that have been impacted by the civil unrest in Minnesota, and helping these businesses is a good thing, and $5 million to YMCA Equity Innovation Center of Excellence. UnitedHealth), and Peloton ($500,000 to the NAACP Legal Defense Fund and encourages other to donate to the Black Lives Matter cause).[136]

With all of these corporation supporting BLM by either giving them money directly, giving money to groups that BLM approves of, or by giving BLM a platform to promote their cause, is it any wonder that they are global and as big as they are, even though they have only been around for six years? With such powerful benefactors, how can anyone believe that BLM is a grassroots movement? Truth is, BLM is not grassroots, they are a very powerful organization that spans the globe and wants to transform America to their vision, and they are succeeding because of the companies named above who support them and their cause, but they are also succeeding because of us. We shop at those companies and we have done nothing to stop BLM when it became evident that they are violent. If you want to know why BLM is able to influence politicians and schools, look at the list of benefactors.

# Media Compliance

*The press should be not only a collective propagandist and a collective agitator, but also a collective organizer of the masses.* —Vladimir Lenin

Besides having support from big name corporations, BLM also has support from the mainstream media (MSM). Not once does anyone on CNN, MSNBC, ABC, CBS, NBC, CNBC, or any of the major networks ever criticize BLM. When BLM activists destroyed Ferguson, Missouri, the media had nothing but praise for them. As BLM activists, mixed with Antifa, destroy cities nationwide, the media insists on calling them protestors who have legitimate grievances, and they criticize anyone who dares to call them rioters, which is what BLM is. Even the few conservative hosts at Fox News refuse to call the BLM activists that are busy looting, burning, and physically attacking other people rioters, preferring to use the word protestor. BLM doesn't need to worry about promoting their own propaganda because there is a willing news media that does it for them.

Anyone who dares to stand up to the BLM thugs are immediately smeared by the media and called racist. The MSM goes out of its way to make sure that you know just how horrible anyone is who would dare stand up to a communist group like BLM. So, what if they deface statues, tear down statues, and vandalize property, or murder someone; BLM is nothing more than a peaceful organization that is fighting for racial justice and racial equity, or so the media tells us, while ignoring BLM's Marxist ties and tactics and their pledge to overthrow American capitalism.

When a woman painted over a BLM mural in the San Francisco Bay area, the media immediately criticized her and made sure that you knew she was white and a Trump supporter, because she had a MAGA hat on. They called her a vandal for daring to stand up to BLM and its movement; never mind the hypocrisy, since the same media sees no problem with BLM activists breaking into business and stealing anything they can find. In Martinez, which is in the San Francisco Bay area, BLM attained a permit to paint a gigantic mural in the middle of a road. A couple, deciding that they didn't want the BLM movement in their neighborhood, painted over the mural, while saying that they were sick of the narrative and wanted it to stay in New York. They were arrested by police and charged with a hate crime.[137] Notice the irony here. The same media that agrees that the police should be defunded so as to fight racism, were thrilled when the same police they want defunded arrested a couple for painting over a BLM mural.

Consider the USA Today headline: "A white man, woman vandalized a Black Lives Matter mural on July 4, called racism 'a leftist lie,' California police say".

Or this one form TMZ: "Trump Supporters Who Painted Over 'BLM' Mural ID'd by Cops, Charges on the Table".

Notice how they make sure that you know the couple was white and Trump supporters? Doesn't anyone find it a bit strange, and biased, that the media is enraged by the vandalization, if you can really call it that, of a BLM mural that was only a couple of weeks old, yet are completely unconcerned about statues of our founders or heroes that have been around for more than 100 years are torn down by anarchists?

When Hawk Newsome, a leader at BLM went onto Fox News and said, "If this country doesn't give us what we want then we will burn down the system and replace it",[138] no one in the MSM seemed concerned about it at all. The same activist finished his interview with the words, "I just want black liberation and black sovereignty, by any means necessary." Did anyone in the MSM find this disturbing or see the connection between his words and the Black Liberation Movement and communist movements worldwide? No. Instead, they ignored the words of Newsome and attacked the anchor for trying to paint him as a radical.

CNN's Don Lemon fired back when his guest Terry Crews mentioned that BLM doesn't focus on the real problems plaguing the black community. When Crews mentioned that black on black crime is more of a problem than police brutality, how more blacks are killed in Chicago and Atlanta because of the actions of other blacks, and how BLM has done nothing to help solve these issues, Lemon criticized him for such an assertion, saying, "What does that have to do with equality, though, Terry? I don't understand what that has to do with equality."[139]

In the same segment, Lemon admitted that BLM only

cares about police brutality and finished up, saying, "If you want an all Black Lives Matter movement that talks about gun violence in communities, including black communities, then start that movement."[140]

Wait a minute. I thought BLM was concerned about saving black lives. That is what we are told they promote: blacks for blacks and the saving of black lives. But as always with Marxist groups there is a stipulation: they only care about a political agenda, and if you get in their way, they target you. What Don Lemon ended up doing is admitting what critics of BLM have always pointed out: that BLM does not care about black lives, or any lives for that matter, but about their political agenda, which for now, centers around eradicating local police forces. Lemon also displayed media hypocrisy and how they will do anything to defend BLM, even when the truth about the organization is right in front of their nose.

When there was a slight surge in COVID19 cases after the July Fourth weekend, the media was quick to blame President Donald Trump's rally at Mount Rushmore in South Dakota, quick to blame any state that didn't have a mask mandate, quick to blame all those who didn't follow social distancing or mask wearing guidelines, and quick to blame all the people who held parties to celebrate the Fourth. But when people pointed out that for over six weeks BLM and Antifa rioters have been gathering by the thousands, many of whom are moving from state to state and who are not distancing themselves or wearing masks, might have played a major role in the uptick in COVID19 cases, the media cried bigotry. For over six weeks, no one in the media bothered to chastise BLM members, or Antifa either, who gathered in large groups to tear down statues, destroy businesses, steal from those businesses, throw Molotov cocktails on cars, attack cop cars, attack cops, pull truckers from their trucks and beat them half to death, or set large fires in the streets. No, instead, the media called them "peaceful protestors" and chewed out anyone who dared to call them what they are: a riotous mob bent on destruction, murder, and mayhem.

Nope. According to the MSM, the uptick in COVID19 cases were all Trumps', and consequently, all conservatives' fault. This is the same media that trashed, criticized, and basically accused any one protesting the mask mandates and the lockdowns back in May of wanting to kill grandma.

While criticizing Trump's rally for helping to spread the coronavirus, NBC conveniently forgot about the praise they lavished on a "black trans lives" event, associated with BLM since BLM also promotes black trans and queer people, and even shared a tweet with a photo showing the thousands of demonstrators that had gathered in front of the Brooklyn Museum. The tweet, read," As the country rallies behind dismantling racist systems that put Black lives at risk in the wake of George Floyd's death, activists have also put a lens on Black trans people who are at the intersection of two dangerously marginalized groups."[141]

But when Trump announced his plans for a July Fourth rally, NBC had a completely different tone, "President Trump plans to rally his supporters next Saturday for the first time since most of the country was shuttered by the coronavirus." Continuing with, "But health experts are questioning that decision."[142] They even had the gall to say, "Large in-person gatherings where it is difficult for individuals to remain spaced at least 6 feet apart and attendees travel from outside the local area."[143] And NBC was very concerned about how these gatherings may cause people to spread the disease to others in their household. Where was their concern about the spread of COVID19 at the "black trans lives" event? Simple. NBC believes in the right of "black trans lives" individuals to get together, but not in the right of anyone who supports Trump to gather.

When a single mother was murdered in front of her fiancé by BLM activists, no one at CNN, Fox News, or any other major media outlet reported it.

But when riots broke out in Charlottesville, Virginia between white supremacists and Antifa, CNN, and other news outlets, were quick to blame the white supremacists for the entire affair, especially when one hit a woman with his car, thus killing her, and made sure you knew who the villains were.

Double standard.

It's no wonder BLM seems to be winning the cultural war, with an entire media supporting them and all too willing to spread their message. The new media in the U.S. is very biased and openly supports left-wing causes. They always have. But we also know what happens when anyone criticizes BLM: they either lose their job, and in some cases their life, making it where a willing media falls in line.

# Political Allies

*"The receptivity of the masses is very limited, their intelligence is small, but their power of forgetting is enormous. In consequence of these facts, all effective propaganda must be limited to a very few points and must harp on these in slogans until the last member of the public understands what you want him to understand by your slogan." —Adolf Hitler*

BLM's list of powerful allies continues to grow as Democrat politicians insist on supporting them, despite the fact that they are nothing more than a black supremacist terrorist group hell bent on destroying America so that they can remake it in their image. These same politicians see no problem with BLM's tactics as they try to achieve their goal where Marxism reigns supreme. Of course, many of these same politicians are Marxists, or socialists themselves, so it should come as little surprise that they support the likes of BLM. They also support Antifa, which is another Marxist organization that is well-funded by George Soros.

One such supporter of BLM is the current mayor of New York City, Bill de Blasio. Mayor de Blasio decided to okay a series of BLM murals to go up in New York City, even though his city has the highest number of COVID 19 cases and deaths, despite the mandated mask order and lock downs, and crime is up at an exponential rate because of his initiative to defund the NYPD. Instead, de Blasio has decided that painting BLM murals around the city is more important, and he helped paint one mural that went in front of Trump tower.[144] Putting the mural in front of Trump Tower was a political tit for tat for de Blasio as everyone knows that Trump and de Blasio do not get along. But the real question that should be asked, which most in the media are not asking, is: why is the mayor of New York helping paint a mural with a group of activists that have done nothing but burn down buildings, damage store fronts, loot, murder, attack cops and citizens, and basically turn New York City into a place of complete chaos and anarchy? Why is de Blasio not arresting them? The answer is simple. Mayor de Blasio believes in the BLM cause because he is also a socialist.

Bill de Blasio showed complete disdain for private property, a common trait among socialists, in an interview once.

> "What's been hardest is the way our legal system is structured to favor private property. I think people all over this city, of every background, would like to have the city government be able to determine which building goes where, how high it will be, who gets to live in it, what the rent will be. I think there's a socialistic impulse, which I

*hear every day, in every kind of communi-*
*ty, that they would like things to be planned*
*in accordance to their needs. And I would,*
*too. Unfortunately, what stands in the way*
*of that is hundreds of years of history that*
*have elevated property rights and wealth to*
*the point that that's the reality that calls the*
*tune on a lot of development....*

*"Look, if I had my druthers, the city govern-*
*ment would determine every single plot of*
*land, how development would proceed. And*
*there would be very stringent requirements*
*around income levels and rents. That's a*
*world I'd love to see, and I think what we*
*have, in this city at least, are people who*
*would love to have the New Deal back, on*
*one level. They'd love to have a very, very*
*powerful government, including a federal*
*government, involved in directly addressing*
*their day-to-day reality."*[145]

Add to this the fact that ever since he drastically cut funding for the NYPD, catering to the demands of BLM, the murder rate in NYC went up by 79%, shootings are up by 64%, and
burglaries are up by 34%.[146] Mayor de Blasio shows no concern
that his city looks more like a war zone than a peaceful city in
a first world nation, so it should come as no surprise that he
not only supports BLM, but is allowing them to graffiti the city.

When asked about the tearing down of a Christopher
Columbus statue in Baltimore, Nancy Pelosi (Democrat Rep-

resentative from California) said, "People will do what they do."[147] Now compare that statement to when the Tea Party held a peaceful protest in Washington D.C. to protest the passage of Obamacare (AKA the Affordable Care Act, which is really the not so affordable care act), she called them "Astroturf". In Nancy Pelosi's world, peaceful protestors that disagree with her are Astroturf, while rioters who burn down cities, but also happen to be Marxists, are just people "doing what they do". It should come as little surprise that she doesn't care that the statues commemorating American history are being torn down. She ordered the removal of Confederate statues in the capital building to be taken down, though I am certain her goal is to tear down all the statues.

BLM activist Monica Cannon-Grant has found favor with Democrat politicians such as, Democrat Senator Elizabeth Warren (the white woman who pretended to be American Indian during her entire career and, ironically, BLM has no problem with that), Boston Mayor Marty Walsh, and Representative Joe Kennedy. She is trying to get Rep. Ayanna Pressley (D) and District Attorney Rachael Rollins(D) re-elected. Monica Cannon-Grant is a staunch racist, who loathes white people and even released a video rant where she trashed Republican Rayla Campbell for marrying a white man. In her rant, Cannon-Grant says,

> *"If white vagina and white penises jeopardize your melanin, then we need you to sit in the back of the classroom. You don't get to talk right now.*

> *"Regardless of many educated gang symbols*

> *you have at the end of your name, regard-*
> *less of how close in proximity you are to*
> *white supremacy, regardless of how many*
> *white penises you ride, just don't forget, that*
> *you's a ni\*\*a.*
>
> *"Keep your mouth shut on black s\*\*t if you*
> *ain't ready to be black... I need you to shut*
> *the f\*\*k up"*[148]

Even the Democratic candidate for president, Joe Biden, in this 2020 election has thrown his support behind BLM. Joe Biden has decided to go full blown Marxist by siding with admitted Communist Bernie Sanders (D), admitted socialist Alexandria Ocasio-Cortex (D), and socialist Pete Buttigieg (D) and has vowed to make mask wearing mandated nationally; to defund the police across the nation; to basically get rid of the First and Second Amendments; and the Constitution and Bill of Rights at the same time; to implement the Green New Deal and kill the fossil fuel industry that allows you to have electricity and running water; to give reparations to blacks by increasing taxes on white citizens and white owned businesses; to remake America's suburbs so that they are more "fair", but basically they are too white in his view; and to take property away from Americans to give back to various American Indian tribes. Read the *Unity Task Force* document that was written by Ocasio-Cortez and Sanders if you want to know Biden's, and the Democrat Party's, entire platform. It may seem strange for a presidential candidate to wholeheartedly support a group like BLM, but Joe Biden has vowed to fundamentally change America, much like Barack

Obama did in 2008, but has anyone asked what he means by fundamentally transform?

And, here is another dirty little secret about Black Lives Matter, the money that is donated directly to them through their website goes to Act Blue[149], which is an organization that funnels money to Democrat campaigns; Joe Biden's being their top priority right now. Act Blue allows Democrat candidates and left-wing groups to raise funds without having to set up an actual donation page. Could BLM just be using a free source to raise money for themselves? Possibly. But, why would an organization that is not supposed to be political and is supposed to be grassroots be using a known fundraising company that is used by the far left for far left causes? Then, there is the fact that Act Blue is able to dole out money in lump sums, but does not have to disclose who they give the money to, so there is no way to verify if the money you donate to BLM, through Act Blue, is actually going to BLM, or something else.

> "ActBlue Charities and ActBlue Civics file Form 990 reports with the IRS, meaning that their top-line finances are publicly disclosed. (ActBlue PAC is governed by the Federal Election Commission and so files different reports.) In 2018 (the latest year available), ActBlue Charities reported almost $24 million in revenues and ActBlue Civics took in an impressive $49 million.

> "But nearly all the money ActBlue Charities and ActBlue Civics paid out is reported

> *generically in one lump, as "passed-through*
> *contributions"—meaning those ActBlue*
> *nonprofits **don't have to disclose** [empha-*
> *sis added] which groups they passed mon-*
> *ey to or how much each group received in*
> *total."[150]*

This is what is called "dark money", or rather, untraceable money, something many Democrats and leftist pundits claim to be against.

Here is another nice little tidbit about ActBlue. One of their groups, ActBluse Civics filled out a 990 Form for their 2018 donations which stated,

> *"Developed online fundraising tools and*
> *methods, trained and educated fundraisers,*
> *and accepted **228,045 pass-through con-***
> ***tributions totaling $45,878,740 for 649***
> ***organizations** from grassroots supporters*
> *[emphasis added]."[151]*

As someone pointed out, 649 groups were given money, but we don't know who they are because they did not have to be disclosed. With almost $46 million contributed by 228, 045 donors, that works out to roughly $200 per person. The Federal Election Commission has set a $200 limit that can be donated to political campaigns by individuals, and if a person donates directly to a campaign, their name has to be recorded. If a person donates to an organization, such as, ActBlue, they can do so anonymously and that money will get passed on without anyone knowing that they, though indirectly, contributed to a political campaign. Is there anyway to prove that this is going on when people donate to BLM? Unfortunately, unless you can get ahold of ActBlue's books, there is no way to prove it, but it is an interesting coincidence and proves that you need to be very careful when donating money to any organization, because you never know where that money will go. However, considering that BLM is a political activist group with their own political platform, and that same platform has now been incorporated into the Democratic Party platform and into the platform of key Democrat leaders, I am willing to conjecture that BLM is really funneling money to certain candidates as a way to increase their political clout.

Either way, none of this changes the fact that Joe Biden, who used to be against defunding the police, has done a complete 180, and is for everything that Black Lives Matter wants. If Joe Biden wins the presidency, BLM, a group formed by Marxists, with have an ally in the White House and an untold amount of influence on American policy going forward.

In addition to a presidential hopeful, BLM also has the support of "the squad": Alexandria Ocasio-Cortez, Ilhan Omar, Rashida Talib, and Ayanna Presley. These four freshman Congresswomen have made it clear that they despise the United States and want to tear down the U.S. economy and remake it into some sort of socialist nightmare. Ayanna Presley has made it clear that she despises whites, and despises blacks who do not think like her, saying,

> *"This is the time to shake that table. ... We*
> *don't need any more brown faces that don't*
> *want to be a brown voice. We don't need*

*any more black faces that don't want to be a black voice."*[152]

Basically, you're not black if you don't support the same left-wing causes as her. Presley has promoted the BLM platform since she entered office, demanding equality of outcome instead of equality before the law. She basically wants to dismantle the system, which is inline with what BLM wants, and she is a powerful ally in Congress, and one the media listens to.[153]

Ilhan Omar has said that she wants to dismantle the system of oppression,[154] which basically means just tearing down the U.S. economic system and replacing it with something of her choosing. On the surface, it sounds good, but she doesn't mean ending inequality. She doesn't care about the disadvantaged any more than BLM does, but she is willing to promote the BLM cause. BLM is already tearing down the system as they burn, loot, and murder, and many who are being harmed by their antics are blacks, especially ones in poor communities, all of whom live in democrat run districts. Omar wants to continue that work by remaking the U.S. economy into what she thinks is fair. What will actually happen is the poor will become poorer, the middle class will disappear, and the wealthy, like her and her Democrat comrades, will remain wealthy. She says that America has a system of oppression, echoing BLM's mantra that America is racist and oppressive to people of color, but Omar is a Muslim immigrant from Somalia, who is also black, and has managed to become a member of the U.S. Congress. If that's oppression, sign me up.

No group gains such political power without powerful political supporters, and BLM is no different on this account.

# Celebrity Endorsements

*"All propaganda must be confined to a few bare necessities and then must be expressed in a few stereotyped formulas... Only constant repetition will finally succeed in imprinting an idea upon the memory of a crowd." —Adolf Hitler*

With all of the support BLM garners, it is little surprise that they also get celebrity endorsements. After all, no amount of support is complete without celebrities in your corner. Celebrities, such as, John Cusak, Tessa Thompson, Kendrick Sampson, Halsey, Jamie Foxx, Chrissy Teigen, Ariana Grande, Emily Ratajkowski, Tinashe, and Nick Cannon, all support BLM, and that is just for starters.[155] For the most part, Hollywood and other celebrities were quick to get on the Black Lives Matter bandwagon to show how "woke" and how anti-racist they are. Like the political supporters and media, they ignore all of the violence that BLM has caused and continues to participate in, choosing to either make excuses, or call any critics of BLM right-wing racists who are part of the KKK. The irony of calling any who disagree with them members of the KKK is truly lost on these people. For those of you who are unaware, the Ku Klux Klan was started by democrats who wanted to keep Jim Crow legislation, again, enacted by Democrats, in effect. In addition, the irony of BLM supporting Democrat candidates is also lost on BLM supporters, considering the Democrat party has always been the party of slavery, are responsible for Jim Crow, were against segregation, and whose policies keep the black, and all poor, communities impoverished.

In the case of Nick Cannon, former host of *America's Got Talent* and host of *The Masked Singer*, he chose to go on an antiwhite and antisemitic rant about how whites are animals. In a rant he did on his podcast "Cannon's Class", Cannon likened whites and Jews to barbaric animals, because according to him, blacks are the true Semites, which is the belief of the Nation of Islam.

> *"When you have a person who has the lack of pigment, the lack of melanin that they know they will be annihilated, therefore they know that however they got the power, they have a lack of compassion, melanin comes with compassion," he began.*[156]

But it gets better.

> *"Melanin comes with soul, that we call it soul, we soul brothers and sisters, that's the melanin that connects us so the people that don't have it, are, and I'm going to say*

*this carefully, are a little less and where the term actually comes from, and I'm going to bring it back around to Minister Farrakhan, where they may not have the compassion."*[157]

And even better.

*"When they were sent to the Mountains of Caucasus, they didn't have the power of the sun. The sun started to deteriorate them. So, they're acting out of fear, they're acting out of low self-esteem, they're acting out of deficiency, so therefore the only way they can act is evil."*[158]

And so on.

*"They have to rob, steal, rape, kill and fight in order to survive. So these people who didn't have what we have, and when I say 'we,' I speak of the melinated people, they had to be savages, they had to be barbaric because they're in these Nordic mountains, they're in these rough torrential environments, so they're acting as animals, so they're the ones closer to animals, they're the ones that are actually the true savages.*[159]

*"So I say all that to say the context when we speak of 'Jewish people,' white people, Europeans, the Illuminati — they were do-*

*ing that as survival tactics to stay on this planet,"*[160]

In response to the outcry following Nick Cannon's rant, ViacomCBS fired him but Fox chose to keep him on the *The Masked Singer.* Cannon did apologize for his words in a series of tweets, but he only apologized for the antisemitic part of his rant, not for the antiwhite sentiments he expressed.

> *First and foremost I extend my deepest and most sincere apologies to my Jewish sisters and brothers for the hurtful and divisive words that came out of my mouth during my interview with Richard Griffin.*[161]

In a statement to the press, ViacomCBS said,

> *"ViacomCBS condemns bigotry of any kind and we categorically denounce all forms of anti-Semitism. We have spoken to Nick Cannon about an episode of his podcast Cannon's Class on YouTube, which promoted hateful speech and spread anti-Semitic conspiracy theories. While we support ongoing education and dialogue in the fight against bigotry, we are deeply troubled that Nick has failed to acknowledge or apologize for perpetuating anti-Semitism, and we are terminating our relationship with him. We are committed to doing better in our response to incidents of anti-Semitism,*

*racism, and bigotry. ViacomCBS will have further announcements on our efforts to combat hate of all kinds.*"[162]

Notice how ViacomCBS is only upset about the antisemitic portion of Cannon's rant, but have failed to mention the bigotry he showed to whites. There is growing antiwhite sentiments throughout the country, pushed by BLM, groups like them, and their followers, and even celebrities and Hollywood are okay with it. In fact, BLM didn't seem to see a problem with Cannon's statements at all. The founder of Black Lives Matter SC, Lawrence Nathaniel, defended Nick Cannon, saying that he agreed with his statements. [163]

It's not just Nick Cannon that is a supporter of BLM, the list of celebrities supporting them, or their cause, continues (the list come from *Need to Know*): [164]

- Michael Jordan (NBA star) giving $100 million to various social justice organizations.
- J. J. Abrams (Director) and Bad Robot, giving $10 million to Black Lives Matter and other racial justice organizations.
- K-pop group BTS, giving $1 million to Black Lives Matter.
- Jennifer Aniston(Actress), giving $1 million to Color of Change and other organizations.
- Rapper The Weeknd, giving $500,000 to Black Lives Matter, National Bailout, Know Your Rights Camp.

- Chrissy Teigen (Model) and John Legend (Singer), giving $200,000 to various bail funds.
- Angelina Jolie (Actress), giving $200,000 NAACP Legal Defense Fund.
- Ryan Reynolds and Blake Lively (Actors), giving $200,000 to the NAACP Legal Defense Fund.
- Cast of Brooklyn-Nine-Nine, giving $100,000 to National Bail Fund Network.
- Megan Thee Stallion (Rapper), giving, $10,225.26 to Restoring Justice.
- Drake (Singer), giving $100,000 to National Bail Out Fund.
- G-Eazy, (Rapper), giving $2,000 to People's Breakfast Oakland.
- Janelle Monae (Actress/Singer), giving $1,000 to the Minnesota Freedom Fund.
- Don Cheadle (Actor), giving $1,000 to the Minnesota Freedom Fund
- Steve Carell (Actor), giving $1,000 to the Minnesota Freedom Fund.
- Kali Uchis (Singer), giving $1,000 to the Minnesota Freedom Fund.
- Seth Rogen (Actor), giving more than $1,000 to various bail funds.
- Kehlani (Singer), giving $1,000 to the Minnesota Freedom Fund.

- Josh and Benny Safdie (Filmmakers), giving $1,000 to the Minnesota Freedom Fund.
- Patton Oswalt (Comedian/Actor), giving $1,000 to the Minnesota Freedom Fund.
- Cynthia Nixon (Actress), giving $1,000 to the Minnesota Freedom Fund.
- Nick Kroll Comedian), giving $1,000 to the Minnesota Freedom Fund.
- Pete Holmes (Comedian), giving $1,000 to the Minnesota Freedom Fund.
- Noname (Singer), giving $1,000 to the Minnesota Freedom Fund.
- Jameela Jamil (Actress), giving $1,000 to the Minnesota Freedom Fund.
- Ben Schwartz (Actor/Comedian), giving $1,000 to the Minnesota Freedom Fund.
- Leonardo DiCaprio (Actor), giving an undisclosed amount to Color for Change, NAACP, Fair Fight Action, Equal Justice Initiative.
- Rihanna (Singer), giving and undisclosed amount to the Color Of Change and Movement For Black Lives.
- Taylor Swift (Singer). Giving an undisclosed amount to the NAACP Legal Fund.

- Harry Styles (Singer), giving an undisclosed amount to various bail funds.
- Halsey (Singer), giving and undisclosed amount to various bail funds.
- Lady Gaga (Singer), giving an undisclosed amount to Black Lives Matter, the NAACP Legal Defense Fund, Color of Change, and more.
- Rob Delaney (Comedian/Actor), giving and undisclosed amount to the Minnesota Freedom Fund.
- Anna Kendrick (Actress), giving an undisclosed amount to multiple organizations.
- Justin Timberlake (Singer), giving and undisclosed amount to the Minnesota Freedom Fund.
- Ellen DeGeneres (Talk-Show Host), gave an undisclosed amount to the NAACP Legal Defense Fund, Black Lives Matter, and the ACLU.

Considering the fact that Hollywood leans left, it is little surprise that celebrities have decided to give to the BLM cause, if not give to BLM directly. Not doing so could get them blacklisted, but many of the above celebrities believe in the BLM cause because they are either unaware that BLM is a Marxist group run by Marxists that want to overthrow the system, or they believe in dismantling the U.S. economy; either way, none of these celebrities will be affected if the economy crashes and will be able to continue to live their luxurious lifestyle.

# Concluding Thoughts

*"Communism is the death of the soul. It is the organization of total conformity - in short, of tyranny - and it is committed to making tyranny universal."* —Adlai Stevenson I

Black Lives Matter has managed to gain a huge following and massive political power in a short span of time, with many unaware of their true origins and goals and many who just don't care. If you are wondering why BLM continues to be a political force to be reckoned with, look no further than yourself. Do you support them? Have you bothered to stand up to them if you disagree with them?

One of the reasons BLM has a massive following is because they appeal to the most basic emotions and carnal nature of humanity. They use anger, jealousy, envy, and hatred to divide people, a common tactic among all followers of Marxism, and it works every time. In just six years, Black Lives Matter has managed to divide the country to the point that Americans are tearing each other apart and burning their own cities.

How do I fight them, you may ask.

Stand up to them. Expose them for who they are. Do your best to not patronize businesses or organizations that fund them, though I realize how difficult that is, since almost all major corporations support them. Do not vote for politicians who support them. But the best way to stop Black Lives Matter, and all followers of Marxism, is to stand united as Americans, united in the belief that individual liberty is for all citizens and that equality before the law is for all citizens. We must quit being divided by petty differences or beliefs based on envy, but be united as individual Americans who appreciate our history,—the good and the bad—who learn from it, and who are grateful for what our Founders tried to give us: a nation based on the idea of liberty for all while living under the rule of law. That is an ideal we have always and must continue to strive for.

Think of America's accomplishments. When we stood united, we defeated European fascism, we won the Cold War, we sent men to the moon, and helped create a world where an individual can video chat with someone on the other side of the globe. I'm not saying we are perfect, but we have always known we weren't, which drives us to be better. If we stand united, as Americans, connected to one another in the common belief that every individual has certain inalienable rights, there is no end to what we, as Americans, can accomplish, and we can be that shining city on a hill. But if we continue to allow totalitarian statists, like Black Lives Matter and anyone who believes as they do, to divide us and tear us down, then America will cease to exist, and the last best hope of mankind will be lost forever. Is that really a world you want to live in?

# Endnotes

1. "Black Lives Matter". *Wikipedia.* n.d. https://en.wikipedia.org/wiki/Black_Lives_Matter
2. Pearce, Matt. "Back Story: What happened in Michael Brown shooting in Ferguson, Mo.?" *Los Angeles Times.* November 24, 2014. https://www.latimes.com/nation/la-na-back-story-ferguson-shooting-story.html
3. "Black Lives Matter organizer stands by group's chant to cook police officers like 'pigs in a blanket' and 'fry 'em like bacon'". *Daily Mail.* September 1, 2015. https://www.dailymail.co.uk/news/article-3217754/Black-Lives-Matter-backs-pigs-blanket-fry-em-like-bacon-chant-Minnesota.html
4. "We Are Trained Marxists" – Patrisse Cullors, Co-Founder, #BlackLivesMatter". Midtown Tribune New. July 3, 2020. https://midtowntribune.com/2020/07/03/we-are-trained-marxists-patrisse-cullors-co-founder-blacklivesmatter/
5. "BLM co-founder Patrisse Cullors was trained by a radical domestic terrorist for more than a decade". *Patriot Daily Press.* June 30, 2020. https://patriotdailypress.com/2020/06/30/blm-co-founder-patrisse-cullors-was-trained-by-a-radical-domestic-terrorist-for-more-than-a-decade/
6. Black Lives Matter. 2020. https://blacklivesmatter.com/our-co-founders/?__cf_chl_jschl_tk__=ed9d-

b62e946717b35bd2abd33211f68bed349c2b-1594566697-0
-ATjzu9uCb6DzlM-cb7XCqMcT999nZYPLnHtk83-JTZ-
rbkIyiXgSEthJMVriD2pzUxZKW6osDTaMaydNAZpB-
PI2rfw3_B3c7E1VBduUPAAI7Q1n-Rpp52KVps4qR-
5jXQp3TB8qsZNZ7l5vyrMx_MwGDHmGovYEnK-
BUmy6eB859M9zBLVx7XurVGIOqOCHLjZIs3x-
3NOii0O8DWzE6GVM283vMfTMJ5vngaMDuloQ-
S6umEvTN-gED3dDvPQwjq9cEDlw_PhE2TCaQg1XnuL-
Vbpb-mIvWqE6eqc99BFeZsHC-Hu44UBczmbn3RfSm-
wM0pqDVHHbA0JKK7H0v1UATRc79jefio88FnPzBb-
jvU6z_M9EL

7    "Dorothy Lee Bolden". *Wikipedia*. n.d. https://
en.wikipedia.org/wiki/Dorothy_Lee_Bolden
8    Shiloh, Tamara. "Black HistoryDorothy Lee Bolden:
Uniting Domestic Workers". *Post News Group*. February 6,
2020. https://www.postnewsgroup.com/dorothy-lee-bold-
en-uniting-domestic-workers/
9    IBID
10    We Dream of Black. 2020. https://www.wedreamin-
black.org/about
11    National Domestic Workers of Alliance. 2020.
https://www.domesticworkers.org/
12    Alicia Garza. 2020. https://aliciagarza.com/about/
13    Black Liberation Movement. 2020. https://blacklib-
erationmovement.com/
14    Valera, Rafael. "Black Lives Matter Founder an
Open Supporter of Socialist Venezuelan Dictator Maduro".
Breitbart. June 13, 2020. https://www.breitbart.com/poli-
tics/2020/06/13/black-lives-matter-founder-an-open-sup-
porter-of-socialist-venezuelan-dictator-maduro/
15    Dowling, M. "Origins of Black Lives Matters". *Inde-*

*pendent Sentinel.* June 13, 2020. https://www.independent-sentinel.com/origins-of-black-lives-matter//
You can read more about the FRSO and its influence on BLM here: https://www.aim.org/special-report/reds-exploiting-blacks-the-roots-of-black-lives-matter/
16      Black Lives Matter. 2020. https://blacklivesmatter.com/what-matters-2020/
17      "Race and Ethnicity in the United States". *Statistical Atlas.* 2018. https://statisticalatlas.com/United-States/Race-and-Ethnicity
18      IBID
19      Black Lives Matter. 2020. https://blacklivesmatter.com/what-we-believe/
20      IBID
21      IBID
22      IBID
23      Talgo, Chris, editor. "What Does Black Lives Matter Want?". *Red State.* June 24, 2020. https://www.redstate.com/heartlandinstitute/2020/06/24/what-does-black-lives-matter-want/
24      Adams, Becket. "AOC: Defund the police means defund the police". *The Washington Examiner.* June 30, 2020. https://www.washingtonexaminer.com/opinion/aoc-defund-the-police-means-defund-the-police
25      The Movement for Black Lives. 2020. https://m4bl.org/policy-platforms/reparations/
The Movement for Black Lives is a political arm of Black Lives Matter.
26      The Movement for Black Lives. 2020. https://m4bl.org/policy-platforms/reparations/
27      The Movement for Black Lives Matter. 2020. https://

m4bl.org/policy-platforms/economic-justice/
28      IBID
29      IBID
30      Engels, Frederick and Karl Marx. "Manifesto of the Communist Party". 1848. pp. 26-27.
31      IBID
32      The Movement for Black Lives Matter. 2020. https:// m4bl.org/policy-platforms/economic-justice/
33      Engels, Frederick and Karl Marx. "Manifesto of the Communist Party". 1848. pp. 26-27.
34      Faddis, Charles "Sam". "The Marxists Are Winning – What Black Lives Matter Really Wants". *AND Magazine.* June 20, 2020. http://andmagazine.com/talk/2020/06/20/ the-marxists-are-winning-what-black-lives-matter-really-wants/
35      IBID
36      "Black Lives Matter demand list wants release all prostitutes from jail". *Pacific Pundit.* June 28, 2020. https:// www.pacificpundit.com/2020/06/28/black-lives-matter-de-mand-list-wants-release-all-prostitutes-from-jail/
37      Read "The Middle of the Road leads to Socialism" by Ludwig von Mises. He explains how Hitler managed to take over Germany and turn it into a socialist country.
38      "Cultural Revolution". n.d. *Wikipedia.* https:// en.wikipedia.org/wiki/Cultural_Revolution
39      "The Black Panther Party". *African America Heritage.* n.d. https://www.archives.gov/research/african-ameri-cans/black-power/black-panthers
40      "Black Panther Party". *The FBI: Federal Bureau of Investigation.* n.d. https://vault.fbi.gov/Black%20Panther%20 Party%20

41      "The Ten-Point Program". *Marxist History: USA: Black Panther Party*. n.d. https://www.marxists.org/history/usa/workers/black-panthers/1966/10/15.htm

42      "The Black Liberation Army and Homegrown Terrorism in 1970s America". *ICSR*. April 12, 2012. https://icsr.info/2012/04/12/the-black-liberation-army-and-home-grown-terrorism-in-1970s-america/

43      Sey, Samuel. "Black Liberation Theology and Woke Christianity". *Slow to Write*. May 5, 2018. https://slowtowrite.com/black-liberation-theology-and-woke-christianity/

44      Bradley, Anthony B., PHD. "The Marxist roots of black liberation theology". *Action Institute*. February 2, 2009. https://www.acton.org/pub/commentary/2008/04/02/marxist-roots-black-liberation-theology

45      Zalman, Amy, Phd. "The Weather Underground". *ThoughtCo*. February 1, 2019. https://www.thoughtco.com/weatherman-aka-weather-underground-3209156

46      Wells, K. "The crazy true story of The Weather Underground" *Grunge*. June 15, 2020. https://www.grunge.com/217954/the-crazy-true-story-of-the-weather-underground/

47      IBID

48      IBID

49      IBID

50      The New Black Panther Party. n.d. https://thenewblackpanther.com/

51      "The Muslim Brotherhood and Black Lives Matter". *The Tribune Papers*. September 28, 2016. http://www.thetribunepapers.com/2016/09/28/the-muslim-brotherhood-and-black-lives-matter/

52      IBID

53       Michell, Lisa. "BLM: Jihad Cloaked In 'Civil Rights' And 'Social Justice'". *America's Civil War Rising*. June 7, 2020. https://americascivilwarrising.org/blm-jihad-cloaked-in-civil-rights-and-social-justice/

54       "The Muslim Brotherhood and Black Lives Matter". *The Tribune Papers*. September 28, 2016. http://www.thetribunepapers.com/2016/09/28/the-muslim-brotherhood-and-black-lives-matter/

55       Aked, Ali. "Arab Social Media Gloats Over Cop Murders in Dallas". *Breitbart*. July 10, 2016. https://www.breitbart.com/middle-east/2016/07/10/arab-social-media-gloats-cop-murders-dallas/

56       IBID

57       Douglass-Williams, Christine. "'Reagan was smarter than you, and he lost!': Iran's Supreme Leader slams Trump, praises Black Lives Matter". *Jihad Watch*. December 28, 2017. https://www.jihadwatch.org/2017/12/reagan-was-smarter-than-you-and-he-lost-irans-supreme-leader-slams-trump-praises-black-lives-matter

58       "The Muslim Brotherhood and Black Lives Matter". *The Tribune Papers*. September 28, 2016. http://www.thetribunepapers.com/2016/09/28/the-muslim-brotherhood-and-black-lives-matter/

59       Koigi, Bob. "Forgotten slavery: The Arab-Muslim slave trade". *Fair Planet*. n.d. https://www.fairplanet.org/dossier/beyond-slavery/forgotten-slavery-the-arab-muslim-slave-trade/

60       "Statements by Hitler and Senior Nazis Concerning Jews and Judaism." n.d. https://phdn.org/archives/www.ess.uwe.ac.uk/genocide/statements.htm

61       IBID

62     IBID

63     Curl, Joseph. "BLM Leader Says Whites 'Sub-Human,' Should Be 'Wiped Out'". *The Daily Wire.*2017, February 13. https://www.dailywire.com/news/blm-leader-says-whites-sub-human-should-be-wiped-joseph-curl

64     IBID

65     IBID

66     Helm, Chanelle. "White people, here are 10 requests from a Black Lives Matter leader". *LEO Weekly.* August 16, 2017. https://www.leoweekly.com/2017/08/white-people/

67     Tuttle, Ian. "More Hypocrisy from Black Lives Matter". *The National Review.* July 12, 2016. https://www.nationalreview.com/2016/07/black-lives-matter-hypocrisy-cheering-violence/

68     IBID

69     Zindulka, Kurt. "Watch: BLM Activist Calls for Revolution in the UK, Saying: 'The Police Is No Different from the KKK'. *Breitbart.* July 13, 2020. https://www.breitbart.com/europe/2020/07/13/watch-blm-activist-revolution-uk-police-no-different-kkk/

70     Hoft, Jim. "Caught on Video=> Black Lives Matter Leader Calls for Running Over, Shooting Police". *The Gateway Pundit.* July 12, 2016. https://www.thegatewaypundit.com/2016/07/caught-video-black-lives-matter-leader-calls-running-shooting-police/
The video can be found on Twitter as it has not been pulled down as of this book's publication.

71     Rugg, Collin. "BLM Takes Over Target: If You Call "The Police" We Will "Shut Your Business Down". *Trending Politics.* June 28, 2020. https://trendingpolitics.com/blm-takes-over-target-if-you-call-the-police-we-will-shut-your-

business-down/
72        Stern, Michael J., "Look at the facts in the Rayshard
Brooks case. The George Floyd killing was different." *USA
Today.* June 18, 2020. https://www.usatoday.com/story/
opinion/2020/06/18/brooks-floyd-deaths-police-miscon-
duct-not-always-racist-column/3206372001/
73        Re, Gregg. "Atlanta mayor calls for citizens to stop
'shooting each other' after murder of 8-year-old near BLM
protest site". *Fox News.* July 6, 2020. https://www.foxnews.
com/politics/atlanta-mayor-calls-for-citizens-to-stop-shoot-
ing-each-other-after-murder-of-8-year-old-near-blm-pro-
test-site
74        Zanotti, Emily. "BLM Protester Will Be Charged
With Attempted Murder After Shooting At Driver During
Utah Protest". *The Daily Water.* July 1, 2020. https://www.
dailywire.com/news/blm-protester-will-be-charged-with-
attempted-murder-after-shooting-at-driver-during-utah-
protest
75        "Karl Marx Quotes". *AZ Quotes.* n.d. https://www.
azquotes.com/author/9564-Karl_Marx
76        "Mao's Cultural Revolution". *Adam Smith Institute.*
May 16, 2019.
77        "Nancy Green, Talented Entrepreneur, Transition-
al Symbol". *Women of Every Complexion and Color.* n.d.
https://womenofeverycomplexionandcomplexity.weebly.
com/nancy-green-talented-entrepreneur-transitional-sym-
bol.html
78        "Karl Marx Quotes". *AZ Quotes.* n.d. https://www.
azquotes.com/author/9564-Karl_Marx
79        "130 Joseph Stalin Quotes That Reflect His
Thoughts On Freedom, Power, War And More". *The Fa-*

*mous People.* n.d. https://quotes.thefamouspeople.com/joseph-stalin-51.php

80    "The Soviet Cult of Childhood". *Guided History.* n.d. http://blogs.bu.edu/guidedhistory/russia-and-its-empires/elise-alexander/

81    Banker, James David. "The Children of the Revolution". *Quillette.* December 18, 2018. https://quillette.com/2018/12/18/the-children-of-the-revolution/

82    IBID

83    IBID

84    Rachmuth, Sloan and Katie Jensen. "Black Lives Matter In Public Schools Is Turning Kids Into Little Marxists". *The America Thinker.* July 8, 2020. https://thefederalist.com/2020/07/08/black-lives-matter-in-public-schools-is-turning-kids-into-little-marxists/

85    IBID

86    IBID

87    Cunningham, Jessica. "Black Lives Matter" *KIPP Philadelphia Public Schools.* June 8, 2020. https://kippphiladelphia.org/about/regional-news/black-lives-matter/

88    Delacroix, Scoops. "First-Grade Teachers In Durham Enroll Kids In Black Lives Matter March". *The Daily Caller.* March 16, 2016. https://dailycaller.com/2016/03/16/first-grade-teachers-in-durham-enroll-kids-in-black-lives-matter-march/

89    Waxmann, Laura. "School board working to put ethnic studies at heart of district curriculum". *San Francisco Examiner.* August 14, 2019. https://www.sfexaminer.com/news/school-board-working-to-put-ethnic-studies-at-heart-of-district-curriculum/

90    Kauffman, Gretel. Philadelphia teachers plan 'Black

Lives Matter week': Does BLM belong in the classroom?".
*Christian Science Monitor.* January 22, 2017. https://www.
csmonitor.com/USA/Education/2017/0122/Philadelphia-
teachers-plan-Black-Lives-Matter-week-Does-BLM-belong-
in-the-classroom
91        "Black Lives Matter facts for kids". *Kiddle.* n.d.
https://kids.kiddle.co/Black_Lives_Matter
92        "The Black Lives Matter At School Coloring Book–
Make this year's week of action beautiful!". *Black Lives
Matter At School.* n.d. https://blacklivesmatteratschool.
com/2019/01/25/the-black-lives-matter-at-school-coloring-
book-make-this-years-week-of-action-beautiful/
93        "Black Lives Matter Week of Action". *Milwaukee
Public Schools.* 2020. https://mps.milwaukee.k12.wi.us/en/
District/About-MPS/Departments/Office-of-communica-
tions-and-school-performance/Black-Lives-Matter-Week-
of-Action.htm
94        Narayanan, Venu Gopal. "The Communist Red
Terror At 100, And Lenin At 150". *Swarajya.* May 23, 2020.
https://swarajyamag.com/politics/the-communist-red-ter-
ror-at-100-and-lenin-at-150
95        "Germany 1933: From democracy to dictatorship".
*Anne Frank House.* n.d. https://www.annefrank.org/en/
anne-frank/go-in-depth/germany-1933-democracy-dicta-
torship/
This site also provides a reading list for any interested in
learning more about Hitler and the Nazis' rise to power.
96        Tham, Engen and Wang Jing. "China launches
political policing task force: state media". *Reuters.* July 6,
2020. https://www.reuters.com/article/us-china-poli-
tics-rights-idUSKBN24804U

97      "Five Reasons Why Che Guevara Is Not Cool".
*Victims of Communism Memorial Foundation*. March 24,
2015. https://www.victimsofcommunism.org/witness-
blog/2018/3/23/five-reasons-why-che-guevara-is-not-cool
98      IBID
99      IBID
100     Foley, Ryan. "School Principal Gets the Boot Because She Was Critical of BLM Pressures in a Facebook
Post". *The Western Journal*. June 22, 2020. https://www.
westernjournal.com/school-principal-gets-boot-critical-
blm-pressures-facebook-post/
101     Davidson, John Daniel. "If You Don't Support Black
Lives Matter, You're Fired". *The Federalist*. June 11, 2020.
https://thefederalist.com/2020/06/11/if-you-dont-support-
black-lives-matter-youre-fired/
102     Bürger, Martin. "Bishop suspends Indiana priest
for criticizing Black Lives Matter". *Life Site*. July 8, 2020.
https://www.lifesitenews.com/news/bishop-suspends-indi-
ana-priest-for-criticizing-black-lives-matter
103     IBID
104     IBID
105     Fairbanks, Cassandra. "Young White Mother Killed
By Black Lives Matter Mob for Allegedly Saying 'All Lives
Matter,' National Media Fully Ignores". *The Gateway Pundit*.
July 11, 2020.
106     Dowling, M. "Former Weather Underground
Leader Handles BLM Funds". *Independent Sentinel*. June 25,
2020. https://www.independentsentinel.com/weather-un-
derground-leader-handles-blm-funds/
107     IBID
If you want to know more about who funds BLM, go to

AIM.org, Accuracy in Media and their article *Reds Exploiting Blacks: The Roots of Black Lives Matter.*

108      Richardson, Valerie. "Black Lives Matter cashes in with $100 million from liberal foundations". *The Washington Times.* August 16, 2016. https://www.washingtontimes.com/news/2016/aug/16/black-lives-matter-cashes-100-million-liberal-foun/

109      GreatGameIndia. "CONFIDENTIAL DOCS: George Soros Funding BLM Style Racial Movements To Topple Donald Trump". *GreatGameIndia.* July 16, 2020 https://greatgameindia.com/george-soros-funding-blm/ You can learn more about the organizations that George Soros funds here: https://realisticobserver.blogspot.com/2017/04/fyi-206-us-organizations-funded-by.html

110      IBID

111      Shaw, C. Mitchell. "The Deep (Left) Pockets of Black Lives Matter". *The New American.* September 5, 2016. https://www.thenewamerican.com/culture/item/23995-the-deep-left-pockets-of-black-lives-matter

112      Richardson, Valerie. "Black Lives Matter cashes in with $100 million from liberal foundations". *The Washington Times.* August 16, 2016. https://www.washingtontimes.com/news/2016/aug/16/black-lives-matter-cashes-100-million-liberal-foun/

113      IBID

114      Randall, Amber. "Ford Foundation Funds BLM-Endorsed Group". *The Daily Caller.* August 10, 2016. https://dailycaller.com/2016/08/10/fortune-500-company-funds-blm-endorsed-group/

115      IBID

116      Wellemeyer, James. "Want to know where all those

corporate donations for #BLM are going? Here's the list.". *NBC News.* June 5, 2020. https://www.nbcnews.com/business/consumer/want-know-where-all-those-corporate-donations-blm-are-going-n1225371

117     Livingston, Mercey. "These are the major brands donating to the Black Lives Matter movement". *CNET.* June 16, 2020. https://www.cnet.com/how-to/companies-donating-black-lives-matter/

118     IBID

119     Togoh, Isabel. "Corporate Donations Tracker: Here Are The Companies Giving Millions To Anti-Racism Efforts". *Forbes. June 3, 2020. https://www.forbes.com/sites/isabeltogoh/2020/06/01/corporate-donations-tracker-here-are-the-companies-giving-millions-to-anti-racism-efforts/#1f18f2f237dc*

120     IBID

121     IBID

122     IBID

123     IBID

124     Wellemeyer, James. "Want to know where all those corporate donations for #BLM are going? Here's the list.". *NBC News.* June 5, 2020. https://www.nbcnews.com/business/consumer/want-know-where-all-those-corporate-donations-blm-are-going-n1225371

125     IBID

126     IBID

127     IBID

128     IBID

129     Livingston, Mercey. "These are the major brands donating to the Black Lives Matter movement". *CNET.* June 16, 2020. https://www.cnet.com/how-to/companies-donat-

ing-black-lives-matter/

130     IBID

131     IBID

132     IBID

133     IBID

134     IBID

135     IBID

136     IBID

137     Culver, Jordan. "A white man, woman vandalized a Black Lives Matter mural on July 4, called racism 'a leftist lie,' California police say". *USA Today*. July 5, 2020. https://www.usatoday.com/story/news/nation/2020/07/05/california-police-white-people-vandalized-black-lives-matter-mural/5381285002/

138     Straub, Steve. "BLM Leader Spills the Beans: 'If This Country Doesn't Give Us What We Want, Then We Will Burn Down The System'". *The Federalist Papers*. June 25, 2020. https://thefederalistpapers.org/us/blm-leader-spills-beans-country-doesnt-give-us-want-will-burn-system

139     Golden, C. Douglas. "Don Lemon Accidentally Destroyed the Left's Racial Narrative with BLM Admission". *The Western Journal*. July 8, 2020. https://www.westernjournal.com/don-lemon-accidentally-destroyed-lefts-racial-narrative-blm-admission/

140     Cost, Ben. "Don Lemon chastises Terry Crews for questioning Black Lives Matter movement". *The New York Post*. July 7, 2020. https://nypost.com/2020/07/07/don-lemon-chastises-terry-crews-over-black-lives-matter-views/

141     Huff, Ethan. "Left-wing media that pushes BLM protests and massive black crowds preparing to blame TRUMP rallies for "second wave" of infections". *Stupid*.

*News.* June 18, 2020. https://stupid.news/2020-06-18-media-blm-protests-crowds-blame-trump-second-wave-infections.html

142    IBID

143    IBID

144    Olson, Tyler. "Trump hits back at de Blasio plan for BLM mural outside Trump Tower". *Fox News.* June 25, 2020. https://www.foxnews.com/politics/trump-hits-back-at-de-blasio-plan-for-blm-mural-outside-trump-tower

145    Boaz, David. "Bill de Blasio is America's Marxist mayor". *USA Today.* September 13, 2017. https://www.usatoday.com/story/opinion/2017/09/13/bill-de-blasios-socialist-dream-david-boaz-column/659138001/

146    Kamioner, David. "NYC murder rate skyrockets under Marxist Mayor de Blasio". *LifeZette.* June 22, 2020. https://www.lifezette.com/2020/06/nyc-murder-rate-skyrockets-under-marxist-mayor-de-blasio/

147    Ferrechio,, Susan. "'People will do what they do': Pelosi dismisses mob destruction of statues". *The Washington Examiner.* July 9, 2020. https://www.washingtonexaminer.com/news/congress/people-will-do-what-they-do-pelosi-dismisses-mob-destruction-of-statues

148    "'White penises jeopardize your melanin': Boston BLM leader and Democrat organizer unleashes RACE MIXING tirade against opponent". *RT.* July 18, 2020. https://www.rt.com/usa/495196-white-penises-jeopardize-melanin-racist/

149    Go to the Donate button on BLM's homepage, scroll down, and you will find where it says that Act Blue handles all donations.

150    Ludwig, Hayden. "ActBlue: The Left's Favorite "Dark

Money" Machine". *Capital Research Center*. June 14, 2020. https://capitalresearch.org/article/actblue-the-lefts-favorite-dark-money-machine/

151    IBID

152    Pollak, Joel B.. "Democrat Ayanna Pressley: No More 'Black Faces That Don't Want to Be a Black Voice'". *Breitbart*. June 14, 2019. https://www.breitbart.com/politics/2019/07/14/democrat-ayanna-pressley-no-more-black-faces-that-dont-want-to-be-a-black-voice/

153    Moran, Rick. "Rep. Ayanna Presley: 'It's Time to Pay Us What You Owe Us'". *PJ Media*. June 27, 2020. https://pjmedia.com/news-and-politics/rick-moran/2020/06/27/rep-ayanna-presley-its-time-to-pay-us-what-you-owe-us-n583089

There is a video interview she did posted here that you can watch where shy promotes the lie of systemic racism and how blacks are oppressed, even though she is one of many black people in Congress.

154    Brenberg, Brian. "Ilhan Omar, others want to 'tear down the system' but real economic equality can only come from this". *Fox Business*. July 10, 2020. https://www.foxbusiness.com/economy/ilhan-omar-tear-down-system-economic-equality

155    Zlotnick, Robin. "Chrissy Teigen, Ariana Grande, and Other Celebrities Who Are Loudly Supporting Black Lives Matter Protests". *Distractify*. May 2020. https://www.distractify.com/p/celebrities-supporting-blm-protests

156    Hasson, Peter. "'Closer To Animals': Nick Cannon Goes On Racist, Anti-Semitic Rant, Says 'White People' And Jewish People Are 'The True Savages'". *The Daily Caller*. July 13, 2020. https://dailycaller.com/2020/07/13/nick-can-

non-podcast-professor-griff-anti-semitic-melanin/
157     IBID
158     IBID
159     IBID
160     IBID
161     Ford, Adam. "Fox will keep Nick Cannon as host of "The Masked Singer" despite anti-white, anti-Semitic rant". *DISRN*. July 16, 2020. https://disrn.com/news/fox-will-keep-nick-cannon-as-masked-singer-host-despite-anti-white-anti-semitic-rant
162     Ausiello, Michael. "Wild 'N Out Host Nick Cannon Fired By ViacomCBS for Failing to Apologize for 'Perpetuating Anti-Semitism'". *TVLine*. July 14, 2020. https://tvline.com/2020/07/14/nick-cannon-fired-anti-semitism-wild-n-out-viacom/
163     Dew, Rob. "Founder of BLM SC defends controversial comments made by Nick Cannon". *ABC Columbia*. July 15, 2020. https://www.abccolumbia.com/2020/07/15/founder-of-blm-sc-defends-controversial-comments-made-by-nick-cannon/
164     "List of Celebrities Who Are Supporting the Riots By Posting Bail for Protesters and Looters". *Need to Know*. June 8, 2020. https://needtoknow.news/2020/06/list-of-celebrities-who-are-supporting-the-riots-by-posting-bail-for-protesters-and-looters/